SETTLER COLONIALISM, SPORT, AND RECREATION

SETTLER COLONIALISM, SPORT, AND RECREATION

JASON LAURENDEAU

First published in 2024
as part of the Sport and Society Book Imprint
doi: 10.18848/978-1-963049-26-8/CGP (Full Book)

Common Ground Research Networks
2001 South First Street, Suite 202
University of Illinois Research Park
Champaign, IL
61820

Copyright © Laurendeau, Jason, 2024

All rights reserved. Apart from fair dealing for the purposes of study, research, criticism or review as permitted under the applicable copyright legislation, no part of this book may be reproduced by any process without written permission from the publisher.

Library of Congress Cataloging-in-Publication Data

Names: Laurendeau, Jason, author.
Title: Settler Colonialism, Sport, and Recreation / Jason Laurendeau.
Description: Champaign, Illinois : Common Ground Research Networks, 2024. | Includes bibliographical references.
Identifiers: LCCN 2024004488 (print) | LCCN 2024004489 (ebook) | ISBN 9781963049251 (paperback) | ISBN 9781963049268 (pdf) | ISBN 9781963049275 (epub)
Subjects: LCSH: Settler colonialism. | Sports--Social aspects--History. | Racism in sports--History. | Discrimination in sports--History. | Ethnic relations--History
Classification: LCC JV105 .L34 2024 (print) | LCC JV105 (ebook) | DDC 306.4/83--dc23/eng/20240412
LC record available at https://lccn.loc.gov/2024004488
LC ebook record available at https://lccn.loc.gov/2024004489

Cover Image: Liz Fox-Grey (artist) ©, Michael Pedersen (photographer) ©

A link to access additional online resources is provided at:
https://doi.org/10.18848/978-1-963049-26-8/CGP

SPORT & SOCIETY POCKETBOOK TEACHING SERIES

The **Sport and Society Pocketbook Teaching Series** aims to introduce students and a general readership to relevant topics, theories, and concepts within sport history and sport sociology. The topics will vary but are united in their purpose to serve as an accessible alternative to generic textbook offerings or academic research monographs. We hope that the shorter and more accessible pocketbook format of the series will mean that each book can be read in an hour or two on a quiet evening or while commuting on a bus or train. This aligns with our ethos of accessibility in scholarly communication.

Books in the series can be accessed in print and electronic formats. In addition, and in parallel to both editions, each title will be accompanied by an online repository where additional learning and teaching resources are provided. The electronic platform for the series will include links to recent and significant research articles, visual materials, podcasts, lectures, and more, thus securing ongoing relevance by providing new and engaging resources and perspectives aligned with the topic of each book.

This series is for teachers, learners, and individuals with an interest in sports alike.

Dr. Jörg Krieger (Aarhus University, Denmark)
Dr. April Henning (University of Stirling, United Kingdom)
Dr. Lindsay Parks Pieper (University of Lynchburg, United States)
Dr. Jesper Andreasson (Linnaeus University, Sweden)

TABLE OF CONTENTS

Acknowledgements vii

Chapter 1: Introduction 1
Chapter 2: Settler Colonialism 21
Chapter 3: Sport, Recreation, and Colonial Violence 49
Chapter 4: Resistance, Resurgence, Reterritorialization 81
Chapter 5: Summary and conclusions 107

ACKNOWLEDGEMENTS

This work simply would not have been possible without the support and teachings offered by numerous students, colleagues, and mentors over the last number of years. In particular, my heartfelt thanks go to Linday Pieper, Jörg Krieger, and the whole editorial team, to the reviewers who offered important and generous feedback and suggestions, and to students from "Sport Recreation, and Settler Colonialism" who have challenged and extended my thinking as we have taken up these topics together. Finally, Carly Adams has supported this work and the personal journey from which it arises in too many ways to enumerate.

CHAPTER 1

Introduction

Introduction

I wonder, reader, how you came to open a book on sport, recreation, and settler colonialism. Perhaps you live in a settler colonial society (e.g., Canada, the United States, Aotearoa/New Zealand, Australia) and are taking a course focusing on sociological dimensions of sport and physical culture. Or, perhaps you are teaching such a course and thinking through how to engage (students) more directly with settler colonialism. In either case, I hope that my work in these pages supports the labour you are undertaking. At the outset, I want to offer a brief but important content warning. In these pages, we will consider some difficult ideas and histories; it is important to sit with the difficulties, the discomforts that these histories and concepts raise. I urge you to consider your capacity and readiness to engage with such ideas, some of which might resonate with your own life experience in challenging ways. I invite you to curate your own reading environment (e.g., where and when you read, taking breaks as they are necessary and restorative, etc.) to best set the stage for the kind of deep engagement I ask of you with this work.

Our work begins with a basic understanding of what settler colonialism *is*. As a starting point, we can understand it as a system that works towards claiming (and reclaiming) lands from Indigenous peoples. That is a rather vague definition to start, and we will elaborate and deepen that understanding in short order. For now, however, I offer a metaphor that might be useful: a spider web. Think of how a spider web *works*. It is composed of numerous thin but delicate threads; together, these threads make for a strong structure that traps those caught in it (the spider's prey). You might think, too, of how a spider web is difficult to see from certain angles, but quite easily seen and felt by those trapped by it. Though the web is strong, it has various weak points; parts of it often fail, dramatically weakening the web. Those caught in the web do not simply succumb to their fate; they do their best to find or create weaknesses in the web as they fight for survival. Lastly (for now), consider the spider, who is simply doing what it needs to do to survive – trapping prey, rebuilding the web as necessary, etc. Whether the spider is "evil" or not is somewhat beside the point for those trapped by the web; they are caught in the web all the same. In each of these senses, the web works rather well as a metaphor for settler colonialism. The "system" I referred to above is not simply one system but rather a collection of systems that work together to form a strong structure – similar to what Woolford (2014; 2015) calls the settler colonial *mesh* or *net* – that targets the lives and lifeways of its "prey" (Indigenous peoples). It is rather difficult for many non-Indigenous peoples to see the system from their perspective and life experience, though much more readily apparent to those targeted by it. Moreover, it shifts and morphs over time and in response to challenges to the system (like the web being repaired). It is by no means a perfect metaphor, but as a starting point, I hope that it gives you a foothold for the work to come. Just as importantly, I hope that this book offers you a different perspective from which to look at the spider web, one that allows you to see the web, how it works, and how the web is both strong and fragile, how it is constantly being made, but also constantly being challenged.

With this initial understanding of settler colonialism in mind, I invite you to consider some questions to help position you for the project of better understanding the contours of this web. What comes to mind when you hear the word "Indigenous" (or "Aboriginal," for example)? Does the word conjure an image of some kind? What about the word "settler"? How do you think the world of sport, recreation, and physical culture is related to these terms?

Too often, when we think of the terms above, we think of "types" of people. In other words, we might think of whether a person has Indigenous ancestry or whether they "settled" in a given territory after moving to "newly discovered" lands from Western Europe, for instance. But these terms must be understood *in relation to one another* and to *systems of power*. Whether I am a settler, for example, is not a question of whether I settled the land or even whether my ancestors did; it is a question of whether I *benefit* from settler colonialism. It is a question, to return to the opening metaphor, of whether the web was built with me in mind. Moreover, the benefits I accrue as a settler are *directly related* to the very real barriers faced by Indigenous peoples on these lands I occupy. It gets more complicated than that, particularly for those forcibly removed from their homelands who now reside in settler colonial contexts, but this, too, is a question of the operation of power.

A recent example might help illustrate the sense in which all of this relates to sport, recreation, and physical culture. The question of Indigenous mascotry (what are sometimes called "Native mascots") is but one entry point into a broader discussion of the interconnections between sport and settler colonialism. The point, for now, is simply that sport, recreation, and physical culture (sport, for short) is a key site of cultural production. In other words, sport is *both shaped by and shapes* broader ideas that circulate in a given society or cultural context.

In 2020, in the context of the "racial reckoning" that followed George Floyd's murder at the hands of Minneapolis Police officer Derek Chauvin, a number of North American men's professional sports teams changed their team names and/or mascots, moving away from often long-standing anti-Indigenous team symbols. In many ways, this represents real and important social change. These team names and mascots have long contributed to anti-Indigenous racism in North America and more broadly (because jerseys, hats, etc. circulate globally), so the changes have certainly gone some way towards harm reduction. The Canadian Football League team now known as the Edmonton Elk, for instance, had an anti-Indigenous team name for decades that stemmed from anti-Indigenous sentiment widely circulating in Canadian society. It also, however, *generated* anti-Indigenous sentiment by widely circulating a term that flattens the realities of Indigenous (in this case, Inuit, specifically) lives, communities, and ways of knowing and being. We could say the same of the National Football League team in Washington, D.C., whose name and mascot directly traded on an Indigenous slur from the early 1930s until July, 2020 (King, 2016; Sharrow, Tarsi, & Nteta, 2021).

Indigenous mascotry also highlights the vital point that these social phenomena and processes are not static; they are dynamic, unfolding, and contested, changing shape in response to social pressures of many kinds (think again of the spider needing to repair the web as threads fray or break). For instance, Cleveland's Major League Baseball team changed the mascot on its merchandise, retiring "Chief Wahoo." In 2022, the team changed its name to the Guardians. These changes came about precisely because so many activists opposed this racist team name and caricature (Jacobs, 2022). This, too, is a key point that I will develop throughout this book. Settler colonialism, as I explain more fully in the chapters to come, is a complex and dynamic system (a network of systems, really), like a network of webs, always in flux, always being reproduced, contested, and/or reshaped.

One final point is worth stressing in this opening example. Settler colonialism impacts the lives of Indigenous peoples, to be sure. But what is often more difficult to see is that it also shapes the lives of settlers in settler colonial contexts. What we will call the settler state (or, in Audra Simpson's terms, the "still settling state") is the cultural, political, and economic context that produces the lives of *everyone* who lives in occupied territories. Whatever our position relative to this *web*, our lives are tied to it in complex, sometimes even contradictory, ways.

Perhaps an additional brief example can help flesh out the point about different lives being shaped by settler colonialism in relational ways. Consider the example of "urban development," as seen through mega-projects such as Rogers Place (a hockey arena) in Edmonton, Alberta. Rogers Place is part of the "Ice District", "a multibillion-dollar sports and entertainment development that opened in 2016 to ensure the profitability of the [National Hockey League's] Edmonton Oilers and to 'revitalize' the downtown core as a spectacular center of consumption" (Scherer, Davidson, Kafara, & Koch, 2021, p. 111). This project entailed a massive influx of corporate and government dollars to "develop" the north-eastern area of Edmonton's downtown core.

Importantly, this process fundamentally changed the lives of both the "urban poor" in these areas of the city and of wealthier classes of Edmontonians seeking recreation and entertainment opportunities, "remarkably chang[ing] how they were able to move, make money, and take up public space in their community" (Scherer et. al., 2021, p. 111). The Ice District provides those with considerable disposable

"Rogers Place" by mastermaq is licensed under CC BY-SA 2.0.

income with new and exciting opportunities to take part in dominant local economies. *As part of this same process*, however, *residents* of this area of downtown Edmonton – disproportionately Indigenous and experiencing poverty – were subjected to new and invasive forms of surveillance. These dramatically limited their activities, including access to social services supporting the necessities of life. At one and the same time, then, the Ice District signaled to many that (this part of) the city is "vibrant" again *and* "has remarkably altered how pre-existing city centre residents are able to inhabit their neighbourhood [as] police presence, surveillance, and harassment... increased with the arrival of the arena" (Scherer et. al., 2021, p. 118). This Ice District thereby constitutes a positive rejuvenation to some and a space of upheaval and harassment to others.

This particular example illustrates Melamed's point "that capitalism is racial capitalism. Capital can only be capital when it is accumulating, and it can only accumulate by producing and moving through relations of severe inequality among human groups" (2015, p. 77). In this illustrative instance, an area of downtown Edmonton was "revitalized" for the benefit of consumers through deepening processes of land dispossession for those already marginalized in a settler colonial context.

Vital Political Work

Learning about sport and settler colonialism is not a neutral or simply intellectual exercise. As I explain more fully below, what we are really considering here is an ongoing genocide (a point I develop more fully in Chapter 2), one with which all of us living in settler states are entangled. As the saying goes, you can't be neutral on a moving train. If, like me, you live in a settler colonial context, you are very much on a moving train. As such, I take an unapologetically politicized and politicizing approach to this topic when I teach it in the classroom; I insist that settler colonialism is genocidal and that we must better understand it *and* figure out how to work towards dismantling it. That same approach informs my writing in this book. As such, I encourage you to approach this work not simply for course credit or out of intellectual curiosity but as part of vital political work against a backdrop of profound and ongoing social injustice.

This is vital political work not in the sense of organized political protest, though that is certainly an important avenue of activist work. Rather, if we accept Lisa Slater's provocative notion that "settler colonialism is a training of the heart," (2020, p. 3), then the work of *retraining* our hearts is key to dismantling this system. In other words, settler colonialism "organizes desire" (Slater, 2020, p. 3), shaping how people living in occupied territories understand themselves, their relationships to each other and the land, and much more. This organization of desire is key to the ongoing political project of settler colonialism. As such, the political work I urge readers to take on (and I am taking on myself) is to *reorganize* desire.

A key question connected to the reorganization I refer to above is *how* to undertake this work. For many working from Indigenous perspectives, the focus is on fostering Indigenous resurgence, desire, freedom, and sovereignty (e.g., L. Simpson, 2017). Those – like me – working in a field sometimes called settler colonial studies, meanwhile, devote attention to understanding the system of settler colonialism in order to better understand and work towards dismantling it. These two broad approaches are not always aligned, as settler colonial studies *can* work to center the lives and desires of settlers and thus gloss over Indigenous strength, values, and ways of knowing. That said, I believe that these two broad lines of inquiry, when approached with care, can be complementary. Certainly, work centering Indigenous resurgence and refusal is vital. Simultaneously, work that calls on those living in occupied territories to better understand their complicity in the overall architecture of the settler colonial project is key. As Leey'qsun scholar Flowers puts it, "settlers have an opportunity to listen, learn, and act in relation to colonial difference *alongside* assertions of Indigenous sovereignty and nationhood" (2015, p. 34, emphasis added).

Importantly, we are talking not only about social injustice but about the kind of social world we want to build. We are talking about the need to dismantle a social world that values profit over people and some people over others, a world that renders lives (of many people, most non-human animals, and the planet itself) expendable in the pursuit of perpetual economic growth. I urge you, then, to undertake this work not out of goodwill but with a focus on creating the conditions for the flourishing of all life, including your own.

With the points above in mind, I invite you to consider your own entanglements with settler colonialism, particularly as they relate to the world of sport and recreation. This is work that has profound implications for our social worlds, so I urge you to approach it as a personal and political project at least as much as an intellectual one. In that spirit, I offer the following questions for you to consider as we get into the heart of the work in this book (I ask many of these same questions elsewhere – see Laurendeau, 2023). These are challenging questions for some of us to consider; I offer them not because they are straightforward but because we will return to them below. I encourage you to take a moment and really consider each question, whether and how it resonates in the context of your life:

- Do you live in what I have called above a still-settling state?
- How well do you know the histories of the lands upon which you reside, live, work, play, etc.?
- Do you know how your ancestors came to be on the lands you now occupy?
- Are you, like me, a white settler? If so, what shape does that take? How does it impact your life?
- Are you a racialized settler, entangled with both white supremacy and your own occupation of stolen lands? If so, in what ways does settler colonialism structure your opportunities, confer benefits upon you, even as you experience institutional and/or interpersonal racism?
- Were you or your ancestors displaced from your homelands by force (e.g., war) more than by choice? If so, how does settler colonialism resonate in your social worlds?

- Are you an Indigenous person negotiating the tensions and violences of settler colonialism on your own peoples' homelands, or perhaps on the homelands of other Indigenous peoples?
- What is your motivation for studying the connections between sport and settler colonialism? Are you simply going through the motions for course credit? Or are you perhaps doing so with an eye towards improving the lives of "others"? Or do you see at this early stage that this is about the conditions that shape *all* of our lives?

These questions are by no means exhaustive, nor is there a *correct* answer to them. Moreover, I do not mean these questions to suggest that readers will fall neatly into one group or another. Some readers, for instance, might have both Indigenous and European "roots" with varying levels of connection to either or both. The point, simply, is that our particular relationships to settler colonialism are likely to be complex and layered. I offer these questions as a signal of the approach I take in this book and the approach I encourage you to take in engaging with it. As I noted above, it may be that you are unsure of how to answer some of these questions. Those in the last bullet point above, in particular, might take time and work to really resonate. For many, it is difficult to see how we are entangled with the structures and practices outlined in these pages, to take up this work as part of a project of building a world that supports life more fully and justly than our world does now.

I hope that the chapters to come will help you engage with these questions with more nuance and complexity. That has certainly been *my* experience in reading, thinking, and writing about settler colonialism; I still have much to learn (and, just as importantly, unlearn).

Situating the Author

It is important to situate myself for readers more fully than I have done thus far. Specifically, I think and write from my positioning as a cisgender heterosexual nondisabled white settler. Here, I point not to some biological realities about my life but to how my identity – my very being in the world – is produced by the systems of power and privilege (e.g., cisheteropatriarchy, ableism) that underpin these categorizations. As I note elsewhere, for example,

> I am "nondisabled" not because I have no (obvious) physical impairments, but because the social structures around me are built to accommodate (and normalize) my particular bodily (in) capacities. My rapidly deteriorating vision, for example, is not a significant barrier to my full functioning at home, work, or play. I am nondisabled, then, in the sense that the world is built with me in mind (Laurendeau, 2023, pp. 27-28).

So, when I write that I am a "cisgender heterosexual nondisabled white settler," I am not hearkening to what is in my blood or DNA, or even to how particular people (e.g., doctors) have classified me over the years based on physical appearance, but to how the social structures around me are built. My "identity," then, is about what these structures make possible in my life, what they render (relatively) easy, the kinds of belonging that I experience because of them, and so on.

Here, it is particularly vital to consider my entanglements with settler colonialism, heeding Macoun's argument that "white settler researchers should approach critical encounters with and through our complicity in ongoing white colonialism, and that this involves attempting to appreciate our own political and epistemological limits" (2016, p. 87). I am, as noted above, a white settler who grew up in Treaty 7[1] territory (Calgary, Alberta, specifically) and have lived, studied, and worked on the lands of many Nations, including those part of the Blackfoot Confederacy as well as Coast Salish, Ktunaxa, Tsuu T'ina, Tsleil-Waututh, Metis, Anishinaabe, and Mi'kmaq peoples. Moreover, many of my family's roots can be traced back through the early days of what is now known as Quebec (and further back, to France). I write, then, from a position of deep complicity in the kinds of colonial violence I describe in these pages. As for my "po-litical and epistemological limits," my position means that I can never know how it feels to live in a system that targets the lives and ways of knowing of me and my loved ones. Moreover, it is not my place as a white settler to speak *for* Indigenous peoples; that would constitute another kind of colonial violence. So, in these pages I make every effort to be clear about "staying in my lane," about my place in making (or not making) particular kinds of claims. This means, for instance, citing Indigenous authors and highlighting Indigenous-led sport organizations and initiatives often.

To return to the question of sport, I will briefly consider some of my own entanglements to illustrate some of the connections developed more fully in chapters to come. My own experiences with sport as a youth involved such things as:

- Attending professional sporting events in which the home team (e.g., the Calgary Flames in the National Hockey League or the Calgary Stampeders in the Canadian Football League) played against teams with Indigenous team names and/or mascots
- Attending the Calgary Stampede, where "Western" culture was celebrated through such spectator activities as

calf-roping or steer-wrestling and Indigenous culture was represented in stereotypical ways
- Attending the 1988 Winter Olympics, an event that was subject to considerable protest by Indigenous peoples and that was rife with anti-Indigenous symbolism
- Singing or hearing the national anthem at sporting events – an anthem that celebrates "our home and *native* land" and produces a sense of belonging to these lands and the country known as Canada that lays claim to them

I will return to several of these examples in the chapters to come, taking up in more detail how they illustrate the interconnections between sport, recreation, and settler colonialism. I also invite you to consider your own encounters with sport and physical activity and ask yourself whether and how they point to these same interconnections. Again, it might be difficult to answer that with any detail at this stage, so I encourage you to keep these questions in mind as you engage with the remainder of this book.

Language

Before we get into the heart of the work, we need to establish some clarity as to the language that we use when engaging with these important topics. Language does not simply reflect social reality; it also produces it. As such, it is imperative that we think carefully about the language we deploy. There is no single "correct" way to refer to the people and processes we will discuss. There are, however, particular effects of using various terms, as I take up below. The language in use is also dynamic and contested, shifting over time in response to various social pressures (including the activism of Indigenous peoples themselves). As such, the brief discussion that follows is a somewhat simplified introduction to these terms and ideas.

Let's start with "settler." This is a hotly contested term in some circles, but is an important marker, as I noted above, of one's entanglements with settler colonialism. As stated earlier, settler colonialism entails building a system in order to lay claim to particular lands and resources. Here, we can add that it is not a one-time theft of material resources, but an ongoing claim to lands and all that can be extracted from them (e.g., oil, minerals, trees, agricultural products, even human remains). In essence, being a settler means benefitting from that system *by choice*. Let's consider me as an example to illustrate this idea. I live in Alberta, Canada because my ancestors immigrated to Canada and "worked the land" in the early decades of the 20th century. They came by choice, worked hard, and made a living for themselves and their descendants. But they did so within a system *designed for them* (and, by extension, for me), one in which the lands they worked were, in effect, *stolen* from Indigenous peoples (more on this in Chapter 2). Generations later, I consider Canada "home" and have rarely had any reason to question my right to be here and move freely on these lands. As noted above, it gets more complicated when we think of people who have (been) moved to settler states by force (especially those whose ancestors were enslaved) or because of violent political upheaval (e.g., asylum-seekers).

Rather than focusing too much on how we classify settlers, I find it useful to heed the words of Flowers, who cautions that the term settler is often employed "without a critical understanding of its meaning and the relationships embedded within it, rendering it an empty signifier" (2015, p. 33). If all we do is simply name or classify (some) people as settlers, in other words, we have missed the point. "The main problem," Flowers continues, "is the reduction of a set of privileges and practices to fit within a binary of Indigenous and non-Indigenous identities rather than thinking through the term 'settler' as a set of responsibilities and action" (Flowers, 2015, p. 33). I look to this quote often as a reminder that the question is not whether or not any individual person is a settler but rather what "responsibilities and action" we should consider as part of our particular entanglements with settler colonialism wherever we live, work and play.

Building from the term settler, let us briefly consider the term "settler state." The settler state refers not to a government formed *of* settlers (though governments in the settler state disproportionately take this form), but to a broader array of institutions and practices all designed in accordance with the logics of settler colonialism. As you will see in more detail in Chapter 2, settler colonialism entails the destruction of one form of social organization and its replacement with another in order to legitimate claims to lands and resources. It is this new form of social organization – not just the government but also, for example, the "criminal justice," child welfare, and education systems – that we invoke every time we use the term "settler state."

Perhaps it would be useful here to return to the metaphor of the spider web and stretch it a little. Earlier, I suggested that the idea of a single web and a single spider might work as a starting point. Here, I want to add a layer or two to this metaphor. You might think of the settler state as a kind of organizational network of spiders. Rather than a single spider working on a single web, imagine an aggregation of spiders working on multiple webs simultaneously, some working closely with others, some working independently without necessarily understanding their place in the network, some not even understanding that they are spiders or building webs (did I mention that we needed to stretch the metaphor?). New webs are constantly being built, older ones being repaired and/or renovated, and some are being torn down either because they've lost their strength or because "prey" are attacking the webs themselves, trying to ensure their own survival.

The point with this metaphor is not to illuminate the specific dimensions of any given settler colonial context, but to point towards the ways in which settler colonialism is dynamic, contested, somewhat but not entirely coordinated, and often misunderstood, even by those doing the work. This is a point to which we will return in Chapter 2.

Next, let's consider "Indigenous peoples." You'll see many terms referring to Indigenous peoples, including terms like "Aboriginal," "Native," "Native American" (a term more common in the United States than in Canada, for instance), as well as several terms now commonly understood as racist. Generally speaking, Indigenous has become the dominant term in recent years when referring to Indigenous peoples in general. That said, it is a contested term, as it homogenizes different and complex peoples and histories. Where possible, specificity is better. If we are talking about Blackfoot or Yellowknives Dene peoples, or Torres Straight Islanders, for instance, then it is prudent to use the specific terms. "Indigenous," however, is a broader term encapsulating peoples with very different histories, cultures, languages, practices, and relationships with various settler states.

Let's look more closely at the term "Indigenous peoples" as you will encounter it or variations of it often in the pages to come. First, note the capitalization of Indigenous. This is absolutely essential. This capitalization "affirms a distinctive political status of peoplehood, rather than describing and exploitable commodity, like an 'indigenous plant' or a 'native mammal'" (Justice, 2018, p. 6). In other words, when we write "Indigenous" we are hearkening not to a *type* of person but to histories, systems of thought, political processes, and more. We are hearkening, in Justice's words, to *peoplehood*, which, as we will see, is so often denied in the settler state.

Next, notice the pluralization of peoples. "Indigenous people" (singular) points to the idea of a *type* of person and refuses the complexities and multiplicity of Indigenous Nations, kinship systems, legal orders, spiritual practices, etc. Peoples (plural) better points towards the very different histories, cultures, and more that are subsumed under a term as broad as Indigenous.

When marshalling the term "Indigenous," it is also important to consider *how* we frame Indigenous peoples in relation to the social world and, in particular, to settler states. The phrases "our Indigenous" or "Canada's Indigenous" peoples, for example, are often heard in political discourse, the mainstream media, and other cultural locations. But these turns of phrase work to refuse Indigenous sovereignty, locating Indigenous peoples within the very colonial structures that have and continue to perpetuate(d) colonial violence. In a different vein, the phrase "the Indigenous" works to flatten the complexities referred to above and, again, to invoke a biological view of Indigeneity rather than one rooted in histories and presents shaped by power structures. As such, these are phrases you will not see me use in this work.

One final note on my use of language in this work: I believe it both possible and important that we engage in these difficult conversations without repeating the slurs that have already done such violence. You may have noticed, for instance, that in the examples of Indigenous mascotry, I did not write the previous anti-Indigenous team names. The use of such terms by Indigenous analysts and commentators is a different matter, one about which I, as a settler, have little to say. Part of my "responsibilities and action" as a settler, however, involves refusing to recirculate these terms that have been weaponized as I write about the connections between sport and settler colonialism.

Keeping Sport in Focus

As we do the conceptual work in this chapter and the next, it is vital to recall that the task in this book is to consider *the connections between* settler colonialism and sport. With that in mind, let us consider one additional example that illustrates some of these connections. In the summer of 2023, the North American Indigenous Games (NAIG) took place in Halifax, Dartmouth, and Millbrook First Nation, all located on lands claimed by Nova Scotia, Canada. This is one of a number of multi-sport festivals organized by and for Indigenous peoples, a phenomenon that has grown since roughly the early 1970s. Events like the NAIG, the World Indigenous Nations Games, or the Arctic Winter Games illustrate the value and importance of such events organized with Indigenous peoples, values, and worldviews at the centre. As Forsyth explains:

> Although the numbers fluctuated over the years, thousands of participants, including athletes, coaches, and mission staff, regularly took part in the games. . . . The largest [NAIG] event for which official data exists was the 2002 games in Winnipeg, in which 4,465 participants from Canada took part. The [NAIG] were established to provide a positive space for Indigenous youth to participate in sport and feel proud of their culture. The mainstream sport system, steeped in white middle-and upper-class values and behaviours, was devoid of meaningful Indigenous cultural content and resistant to change. (2020, pp. 125-126)

Forsyth's words highlight the importance of understanding the "mainstream" sport system as one that is both rooted in and productive of particular ideas (e.g., about "sports," bodies, gender, and more). They also point to the value of Indigenous-led and organized sporting spaces, a point to which I return in the chapters to come. For now, I offer this tether to the NAIG as an illustration of how sport and settler colonialism are intertwined and to point to the idea that Indigenous peoples are not simply *victims* in all of this; they creatively and purposefully resist, refuse, and reimagine life (and sport) in and under settler colonialism.

Outline of the book

After this brief introductory chapter, I offer three main substantive chapters. In Chapter 2, I lay out the analytic contours of the work ahead, explaining the core ideas and frameworks that inform our interrogation of sport, recreation, and settler colonialism. In Chapter 3, I go into greater depth taking up examples of how sport has been and continues to be a site of settler colonial violence. In Chapter 4, I take up sport and recreation as sites of resistance, resurgence, and reterritorialization.

In Chapter 5, I draw together key themes from the preceding chapters and consider the importance of studying the interconnections that form the core of this work. In this final chapter, I consider the question I so often hear in the classroom: "What can we do?" At the same time, however, I argue that there is no instruction manual for this work, no single right way to work against histories and presents of colonial violence, either in our intellectual work or in terms of our lives more broadly. I point towards the idea that we must commit, in an ongoing way, to rethinking and reimagining what we have learned in and from the settler state in all its manifestations. In the context of this particular work, the manifestation that is most relevant is our encounters with sport, recreation, and physical activity. I conclude the book, then, with some examples of how we might engage in the process of *unlearning* much of what we have learned in and through sport.

Discussion Questions

- What does it mean to suggest that we should always think of terms like "settler" and "Indigenous" in relation to one

another and to systems of power? How is this different from thinking of them as categories or types of people?
- How does the example of Indigenous mascotry illustrate the connections between sport and settler colonialism?
- What do we invoke when we employ the term *settler state*?
- In what sense is settler colonialism an *ongoing* project?
- Why is it important to capitalize "Indigenous" and pluralize "peoples" when referring to Indigenous peoples?

CHAPTER 2

Settler Colonialism

What is Settler Colonialism?

How well do you understand settler colonialism? Based on what you read in Chapter 1, what you might have encountered in school, or what you know from popular culture, how would you describe it? Where do we *see* settler colonialism? How does it work? What are the logics upon which it is built? Perhaps these are challenging questions to answer at this point. I invite you to keep them in mind as you engage with this chapter; I hope that by the time you finish Chapter 2, you will have a clearer sense of how to engage with such questions.

In Chapter 1, I pointed out that settler colonialism is a complex and dynamic network of systems, always in flux, always being reproduced, contested, and/or reshaped. I suggested that we might think of a network of spider webs as a productive metaphor for developing our understandings of settler colonialism. Towards what end does this network work? What is the goal, the point of settler colonialism? In short: land. As Tuck and Yang argue: "Land is what is most valuable, contested, required" (2012, p. 5).

To flesh this out in greater depth, it is useful to take seriously Veracini's argument: "Colonialism is not settler colonialism" (2011, p. 1). Veracini explains that "the two stances are often intimately intertwined," that similar ideas and goals are shared, and that it is sometimes difficult to parse the relative positions as different colonial agents might articulate the goals and means somewhat differently even from the same specific (settler-)colonial context. Nevertheless, he points out, the "analytical distinction, and the dissimilarity between the relational systems they establish, remains crucial especially because distinct stances create different conditions of possibility for different patterns of relationships" (2011, p. 2). In other words, the two "stances" set the stage for fundamentally different relationships between colonizers and "the colonized." As such, it is vital to consider the broad contours of each project in order to appreciate the specific logics – and violences – of settler colonialism.

In broad terms, under colonialism, powerful invaders plunder the "resources" of peoples they encounter and return stolen goods to the colonizing country. This requires an ongoing relationship of subordination to ensure a continued supply of goods to accumulate wealth for colonial powers: "in the case of colonial systems, a determination to exploit sustains a drive to sustain the permanent subordination of the colonised" (Veracini, 2011, p. 2). Under settler colonialism, however, invaders *stay*, as the main "resource" is the land (land, in this analysis, is shorthand for lands, waters, and any/all "resources" that might be extracted – e.g., oil, minerals, non-human animals, etc.). Invaders want the land in order to accumulate capital (wealth). So, this is not a one-time theft of material goods, but an ongoing process of capital accumulation that requires ongoing and unfettered access to (i.e., "ownership of") land. Under colonialism, then, the object is to leave a system intact and reap the benefits (e.g., material goods) of it. Under settler colonialism, by contrast, there is "a persistent drive to ultimately supersede the conditions of its operation" (Veracini, 2011, p. 2). The aim, in other words, is to replace the existing people with settlers and the existing social order with a new one, as I elaborate below.

The question of *relationships to* land is absolutely key to understanding the settler colonial project. Specifically, under settler colonialism land and capital accumulation are rendered possible only by framing land as a resource or asset. As Tuck and Yang point out, "…land is remade into property and human relationships to land are restricted to the relationship of the owner to his property" (2012, p. 5). Perhaps, as a reader, you find yourself thinking something along the lines of: "Of course land is property…" This is quite understandable as that is the dominant way of understanding land in many so-called modern societies. It is not, however, the only way to think about land, nor was it how land was understood in territories now claimed by settler states like Canada, the United States, Australia or Aotearoa/New Zealand prior to "contact." Bearing in mind the variations and complexity in and among Indigenous communities, worldviews, etc., we can note one common thread that connects understandings of land within many Indigenous worldviews: Land is not something to be *owned*, something from which resources are to be extracted. Rather, land is seen as an important (perhaps the most important) *teacher*, something to be revered and respected, something to and with which people and Nations have obligations. Leanne Betasamosake Simpson, writing from an Anishinaabe perspective, puts it beautifully: "Indigenous bodies don't relate to the land by possessing or owning it or having control over it. We relate to land through connection – generative, affirmative, complex, overlapping, and nonlinear relationship" (2017, p. 43).

A "New Social Order"

From the invaders' perspectives, people already on desired lands (as well as their systems of governance, justice, spirituality, etc.) constitute barriers that must be removed (and must not be allowed to be rebuilt) in order to gain and maintain access to land. As such, the "horizons of the settler colonial nation-state are total and require a mode of total appropriation of Indigenous life and land" (Tuck & Yang, 2012, p. 5). To put it differently, in the settler colonial project, in order to gain and retain control over lands and waters, settlers and settler states create "a new social order that depends in part on the ongoing oppression and displacement of Indigenous peoples" (Justice, 2018, p. 9). The network of spider webs, in other words, works towards the ultimate aim of claiming lands and maintaining control over them. The new social order built as part of the settler colonial project *is* this network. New institutions (e.g., educational institutions, child welfare and criminal justice systems) are built *as part of the network of webs*. They are built (and rebuilt, and rebuilt), in other words, to legitimate the claims of still-settling states to the lands they occupy.

In some instances, we see this new social order come about during a relatively short period, as in the case of Israel. In the early 20th century, the League of Nations delegated Britain a Mandate to rule over Palestine, ostensibly to ready the people for self-government. Purportedly, Britain's rule would allow for the development of important infrastructure, institutions, and practices that would enable Palestinians to govern themselves in the longer term (Shihade, 2017). As Shihade explains, however, what unfolded in the coming decades was something altogether different (and arguably more sinister):

> ...what the British Mandate government accomplished during its control of Palestine from 1922 to 1948 was, on one hand, a systematic repression of political and economic development of the native Palestinians, and on the other hand, institutionalized support of the Zionist settler enterprise in Palestine. Comprised mainly of European Jewish settlers, they managed to build a semi

> state-like economic, political, and military structure during the time of British rule. (2017, p. 68)

The building of a new social order unfolds in different ways in different settler colonial contexts. This notion of a new social order may sound rather orchestrated, as if it developed according to a specific master plan put into practice at a particular moment in time. As Strakosch emphasizes, though, "settler sovereignty was not simply created in a single act of foundation, proclaimed, desired and established prior to the extension of government over Indigenous lives. Rather… it was asserted in local and specific ways in order to resolve particular questions of order on the ground" (2015, p. 53). We need threads of a web right here, the logic goes, in order to make the lives of people living here more peaceful. It is through the repetition of such moments that the network of webs is built and reinforced.

Strakosch highlights the sense in which the authority of the settler state to govern is not a given, but is produced and reproduced through its own continual assertion. Looking at "Indigenous policy" in settler states in particular, Strakosch argues that policy, "as a performance of the routine ordering of domestic life of the sovereign state, becomes both a powerful assertion that this state is complete, and a site where it is constructed" (Strakosch, 2015, p. 53). The point here is that the "new social order" did not and does not come fully formed. Rather, it arises out of the particular decisions made by those assuming and asserting the authority to govern in settler colonial contexts. These assertions themselves simultaneously produce the settler state and the idea that it is immutable.

Let us consider an example from the world of sport to illustrate this point. One of the many areas in which the settler state sets policy is in terms of funding for various sport organizations and initiatives. Forsyth points out that Canadian government policy in this area has been and continues to be inextricably colonial. Forsyth's work highlights that contemporary government decisions about which Indigenous sporting initiatives are worthy of funding, for instance, draw on the same logic as the kinds of legislation that regulated nearly every aspect of Indigenous lives for decades. In the late 19th and early 20th centuries, the Indian Act banned and criminalized Indigenous dances and festivals that involved gift-giving or physical wounding of participants, arguing that both indicated the primitiveness of Indigenous cultures (Kulchyski, 1992). There is a paternalistic logic at work here – "father knows best" which activities are appropriate and "civilized." Forsyth highlights that the same logic is woven into contemporary sport governance in settler Canada:

> though the ban on traditional religious cultural practices such as the Potlach and Sundance had been quietly removed from the *Indian Act* in 1951, the thinking that underpinned that policy continued through informal measures that provided financial assistance to sport and recreation activities that fit government-approved criteria, thus ensuring that Indigenous energies would be channeled into appropriate physical behaviours. (Forsyth, 2020, p. 87)

The reappearance of these paternalistic logics in contemporary sport funding policy are among the "shape-shifting tactics" of settler colonialism that "may on the surface appear to be subtle [but] like other brutal forms of oppression, threaten the very survival of Indigenous communities" (Alfred & Corntassel, 2005, p. 602). In this example, settler state sport policy – one small web – constitutes part of the broader network of webs (the settler colonial mesh – Woolford, 2015) in numerous respects: It supports and fosters only particular kinds of physical activities – those consistent with ongoing colonial rule; it draws energies away from activities that would (re)generate deep, reciprocal, relational connections to lands; it (re)produces the idea that these decisions are rightly located in the realm of the settler state, again locating Indigenous peoples and their physical activities under the purview of the settler state, which is both seen and produced as legitimate and complete (Forsyth, 2020; Strakosch, 2015).

This "new social order" both necessitates and works towards the "total appropriation of Indigenous life and land" to which Tuck and Yang (2012) refer. In other words, Indigenous peoples need to be removed from the lands (or their claims to the lands rendered meaningless) in order for the new social order to (continually) be built. According to the logic of settler colonialism, the new social order must keep Indigenous peoples separated from their lands and ways of being in relation to those lands. This is yet another sense in which settler colonialism is inescapably an *ongoing* project; it constitutes not a singular claiming of land but an ongoing process of reasserting the rights to own and exploit lands as well as govern, educate, "protect," and represent the peoples of those lands. Moreover, each of these dimensions of assumed sovereignty and authority proceed according to colonial logics. Governance, political representation, education, and protection all cohere with the overall project of settler colonialism.

Education is an instructive example. As Harris notes: "Radical pedagogists and Indigenous theorists agree that the education that all of us, Indigenous and non-Indigenous, receive in schools and universities presumes the dominant Western world view based on positivistic scientific principles" (2002, p. 188). Harris' words point to the importance of understanding not only elementary and secondary school whitewashed curricula, but also institutions of so-called higher education, as implicated in this project. Historically, universities on lands claimed by Canada and the United States emerged as part of the projects of Christianizing Indigenous youth and reproducing settler colonialism through teaching

"Protestantism, the English language, and British culture to the white settler youth of the growing colony" (Hampton, 2020, p. 16). By the early 20th century, in "addition to promoting European classical knowledge, the university served as a site for the development of racial ideology that served to justify slavery and colonization without contradicting European Enlightenment ideas about freedom and equality" (Hampton, 2020, p. 17). This, too, echoes loudly in the present as universities and the disciplines that make them up overwhelmingly center Eurowestern voices, bodies of knowledge, ways of knowing, and axiological assumptions (in short – values). I encourage you to interrogate the course outlines you encounter in post-secondary classrooms. Perhaps you are majoring in kinesiology, sport management, or sociology, for instance. Think of the courses you take as part of your major as well as your electives from other disciplines. Whose voices, perspectives, and knowledge systems are valued, centered, and treated as if they are somehow neutral or objective – as existing outside of power structures? Whose are erased, dismissed as "unscientific," and/or treated as window dressing? What does all of this reveal about (higher) education as an "arm of the settler state" (Grande, 2018)? What does it tell us, in other words, about education as one of the webs?

At this point, it is useful to briefly point towards the justifications for (settler) colonialism. In both the past and the present, colonial occupation is often rationalized according to a logic that colonial rule improves the lives of everyone by bringing "backwards" or "uncivilized" peoples into the "modern present." In other words, colonial apologists hold up the new social order (in a settler colonial context) described above as an inherently worthy aim. For instance, in a highly controversial publication, Gilley argues that on balance, Western colonialism has provided net benefits for people in "underdeveloped" regions, including:

> expanded education, improved public health, the abolition of
> slavery, widened employment opportunities, improved administration, the creation of basic infrastructure, female rights, enfranchisement of untouchable or historically excluded communities, fair taxation, access to capital, the generation of historical and cultural knowledge, and national identify formation. (2018, p. 4)

The fundamental flaw in such arguments is found in their underlying assumptions: that "modern" institutions are both inherently superior to "pre-modern" ones *and* that such "modernization" would not have occurred but for colonialism. As Rodriguez explains:

> A compelling case can be made that colonialism's exploitation of the third world's natural resources and manpower is exactly what has disrupted and undermined the kind of political, intellectual and institutional work that all peoples must do in order to survive and thrive. (2018, p. 256)

Gilley's notion of "expanded education," for instance, hearkens specifically to education reformulated along modernist lines that rationalize particular (colonial) kinds of social organization (Harris, 2002; Simpson, 2014). It's not that education wasn't woven into the lives of Indigenous peoples and communities on lands claimed by Canada, for instance, it's that it wasn't the "right" kind of education (seen through a colonial lens, as described above). Instead, education in Indigenous Nations emphasized relationality, responsibility, and life-long learning with and from the lands, non-human animals, plants, and communities in which people were enmeshed (Harris, 2002; Simpson, 2014). While many of Gilley's claims point to social gains understood by many as desirable, the notion that such advancements only came about because of colonial rule is, quite simply, based on assumptions and speculation rather than compelling evidence. Overall, his work thus suggests "that most third world peoples [are] incapable of achieving certain kinds of development by relying on [I]ndigenous models of development... because of some kind of moral and intellectual deficit" (Rodriguez, 2018, p. 257). The ba-sic argument is this: "modernization could only have come about through modern governance." It is a circular argument in which "modernity" is seen as inherently good, and only possible as a result of "modern" forms of governance. Within this worldview, the notion that "access to capital" is not necessarily a desirable organizing principle of societies, or that historical and cultural knowledge were (and are) continually produced by Indigenous communities – and were and are specifically targeted for erasure by colonial projects – is genuinely unthinkable.

It is also important to note that settler colonialism takes a variety of forms depending on the particular geopolitical context. In other words, *particular* webs are built at particular times in particular places in light of both local conditions and aims. In North America, for example, it entailed European settlers "exploring" what they saw as new territories ripe for development, declaring them "empty" (the doctrine of *terra nullius* – from the Latin expression for "nobody's land"), and subsequently claiming huge swathes of land and fashioning a new nation. In other contexts, however, the process has unfolded rather differently. Consider Hokkaido, Japan, as just one example. The northern-most island of Japan was for centuries known as Ainu Mosir ("the peaceful land of human beings") to the Ainu peoples who called it home (Grunow et. al., 2019). In the 17th, 18th, and 19th centuries, commercial forces from mainland Japan, under the Tokugawa shogunate, developed trading relationships with Ainu peoples in the southwestern parts of Ainu Mosir. Wajin (non-Indigeous Japanese peoples) thought of the northern island as populated by "savages," offering some sense of the racism already fomenting in these years (Hirano, 2015). Waijin subjected Ainu peoples to physical and sexual violence, separated families and communities by sending many Ainu men and women to (different) fisheries to work as corvee labourers, and more. Some observers suggest that this constituted an example of settler colonialism. Others, however, point out that since Ainu peoples were still permitted access to their lands, waters, and forests, the foundational logic of settler colonialism – the claiming of lands and removal of Indigenous peoples from those lands – was not yet evident. This changed dramatically with the onset of the Meiji period in which the capitalist "modernization" of Japan was the driving force. As part of this project, the Meiji government declared Ainu Mosir *terra nullius* and claimed it as part of the new, modern Japan. Meiji Japan then looked to American "experts" with experience "managing" Indigenous populations as they worked to dispossess Ainu peoples of the lands with which they had lived in relation for millennia (Grunow et. al., 2019).

Sámi peoples on lands claimed by Nordic countries provide another example that parallels that of Hokkaido, yet is different in important respects. Sápmi, or Sámi territory, is currently claimed by Norway, Sweden, Finland, and Russia. As these nation-states divided up their territories, Sámi peoples had some of their rights and responsibilities enshrined in law and governance processes (Kuokkanen, 2020). These included movements across borders and approving fisheries along the Deatnu River that formed the backbone of their territories. Until the end of the Second World War, the border between Finland and Norway, for instance, was organized in a way that allowed Sámi to exercise their traditional rights and practices to a large extent without significant interference from either government. Gradually, however, amidst shifting geopolitical tensions and scientific concerns about the stock of salmon in the Deatnu River basin, Nordic nation-states have increasingly assumed governance over these lands and waters (Kuokkanen, 2020). As in the case of Hokkaido, then, we see a process of settler colonialism that shifts and morphs over time, depending on the geopolitical context. In this case, Sápmi was and is at the intersections of several states with ambitions to "develop" the lands and waters for which Sámi peoples have cared for millenia. Kuokkanen sums it up, writing:

> the gradual administrative and political consolidation of state control and authority over several centuries and the concomitant erasure of the Sámi social, political and legal order... is a case of settler colonial domestication and destruction of an Indigenous society in order to replace it by its own. (2020, p. 514)

The point here is not to suggest that there are different *types* of settler colonialism but to highlight the importance of the particular contexts within which settler colonialism unfolds. The logics of settler colonialism are quite consistent. But how those logics unfold *in practice* is a matter of the particular historical, geographical, and social factors in each context.

A "Logic of Elimination"

Settler colonialism is not only an ongoing project, but a genocidal one. As noted above, for the settler state to reproduce its claims to legitimacy and to ownership over lands, waters, etc., Indigenous peoples and their claims to the same lands must be eliminated. It is in this sense that settler colonialism is structured by a "logic of elimination" (Wolfe, 2006). Importantly, this logic is not about targeting Indigenous peoples per se. It is not part of some project of pursuing racial purity. Rather, it is about securing access to lands and resources in an ongoing way: "...the primary motive for elimination is not race (or religion, ethnicity, grade of civilization, etc.) but access to territory" (Wolfe, 2006, p. 388). In other words, Indigenous peoples are not targeted in and by settler colonialism *because of racism*; rather, racism emerges from the perpetual need to reassert claims over lands and resources.

This logic of elimination is not simply oriented towards the elimination of Indigenous peoples but towards their elimination *as Indigenous peoples*. The point, again, is to interrupt claims Indigenous peoples have to the lands, waters, and resources claimed by the settler state. This can be accomplished through the elimination of Indigenous peoples themselves, but that is not the only route to this interruption. The settler state aims to eliminate Indigenous kinship networks, political/legal orders, governance processes, knowledge systems, and more. In some contexts, it also involves targeted efforts to undermine the solidarity of oppressed peoples by recruiting some Indigenous peoples into alliance with the colonizers. We see this in Israel, for example, with the Druze, an Indigenous population recruited to join the Israeli military and educated in ways designed to highlight "links between Druzes and Jews, which has had the effect of downplaying and even erasing the shared history of Druzes and the larger Arab community" (Shihade, 2017, p. 69). It is in this sense that I referred to a network of systems in Chapter 1. For the settler state to target these many dimensions of Indigenous life, for it to work towards the "total appropriation of Indigenous life and land" (Tuck & Yang, 2012, p. 5), requires a constellation of institutions, policies, and practices – a constellation of webs – that work in concert with one another towards these ends.

In the Canadian context, the constellation of webs referred to above can be seen in child welfare (e.g., Lindstrom & Choate, 2016), social work (e.g., Fortier & Wong, 2019), the criminal (in) justice system (e.g., Crosby & Monaghan, 2016), higher education (Harris, 2002; Simpson, 2014), and many more institutional spaces. It is in this sense that Audra Simpson refers not to settler states but to "*still settling*" states (2017, p. 20). Though an in-depth consideration of these institutions is beyond the scope of this particular book, each of them works to interrupt Indigenous lives, lifeways, kinship networks, and/or knowledge systems on these lands. Together, they re-instantiate settler ways of being and knowing as desirable, natural, and commendable. These ways of knowing and being, in other words, are cast not as *particular* ways of orienting ourselves in and to the world, as choices made over time and with real, material, deadly consequences, but as (for example) "Canadian values."

Let us return to the world of sport for a moment to see how this targeting can play out in practice. Both Canada and the United States established residential schools for Indigenous children. Though politicians claimed that the aim of these schools was to educate and "help" young Indigenous peoples, these institutions actually constituted forced assimilation and inflicted extraordinary violence on Indigenous children, families, and kinship systems (Woolford, 2015). Religious institutions were central to the operation of residential schools, but so too were governments, who shared "lessons and information" across the border as they each worked hard to "contend with the so-called Indian problem" (Woolford, 2015, p. 2). The logic of elimination comes through clearly in a famous quote from Sir John A. MacDonald, Canada's first Prime Minister, uttered in the House of Commons in 1883:

> When the school is on the reserve the child lives with its parents, who are savages; he is surrounded by savages, and though he may learn to read and write his habits, and training and mode of thought are Indian. He is simply a savage who can read and

> write. It has been strongly pressed on myself, as the head of the Department [of Indian Affairs], that Indian children should be withdrawn as much as possible from the parental influence, and the only way to do that would be to put them in central training industrial schools where they will acquire the habits and modes of thought of white men. (cited in Stonechild, 2006, p. 9)

Thousands of survivors and their descendants later testified to the Truth and Reconciliation Commission (TRC) how their experiences with residential schooling impacted their lives, loved ones, and communities. Many testified that they were forcibly separated from their parents, were forbidden to communicate in their own languages, were not allowed contact with their own siblings. Even those who did not experience the most egregious abuses (e.g., physical, sexual, etc.) were part of a project famously designed to "take the Indian out of the child."

This is not to suggest that none of those who attended residential schools remember them in positive terms or that there was no kindness to be found in their hallways or classrooms. To return to the metaphor of the network of spider webs, some of those working in these institutions would have approached this work with kindness and benevolence, not appreciating nor understanding, necessarily, that whatever their motivations or dispositions, they were building webs that proved deadly. Rather, the point is that whatever the experiences of particular students, whatever the motivations or dispositions of those (e.g., clergy, nuns, teachers) doing the work, the *architecture* of the program itself is inescapably genocidal. In other words, the residential schooling system was designed to sever the relationships between Indigenous children and their families, Nations, lands, and ways of knowing and being. Whether this work is undertaken with kindness or not, its effects are genocidal.

How does sport come into the question of residential schooling? Many of those who attended residential school facilities fondly recalled their experiences playing hockey or lacrosse, for example, noting that these moments of play provided them much-needed respite from the rhythms and violences of their day-to-day lives in these institutions. For some, then, sport was a life-preserver of a sort, giving them something positive to hold onto amidst the horrors of their institutional lives. This is a critically important point, one it is vital to honour for those survivors who remember their experiences in this way.

While honouring the positive memories of (some) residential school survivors, we can also interrogate the place of sport at a structural level, carefully considering the purposes towards which sport was marshalled by governments, religious institutions, and their agents. Once again, we can and should consider sport as both oppressive and freeing, often in the same lives and particular contexts.

Forsyth (2013) has written compellingly about the place of sport in residential schools. Her work highlights that the overall effects of sport in these spaces are part of the larger project of settler colonialism. The ways school agents organized sport worked to reshape Indigenous children's understandings of and connections to land. For example, the sports deemed permissible taught them the kinds of spatial relations implicit in activities with clearly defined and linear boundaries (think of a hockey rink or soccer field, for instance). This, Forsyth persuasively argues, targets a key element of Indigenous knowledge and ways of knowing; instead of understanding land in *relational* terms (recall Leanne Simpson's arguments here), students were taught to understand land simply as abstract space that can be delimited as needed for recreational purposes (a utilitarian and colonial view of land). In other words, these sporting experiences in residential schools taught Indigenous youth that their own cultural understandings of land were outdated and worked to replace these notions with "modern" understandings of land and space.

Forsyth also describes how students were siphoned into particular recreational activities with the effect of producing understandings of themselves, their bodies, and the Canadian nation that aligned with colonial aims. The emphasis on military drills, for instance, was "designed to replace tribal allegiances with a sense of patriotic duty" (2013, p. 23). Boys and girls were also drawn into the gendered patterns evident in Canadian society more broadly:

> the boys were encouraged to be vigorous and competitive, while the girls were generally provided with opportunities to engage in unstructured, less physically demanding activities. These patterns served to reinforce the notion of competitive sport as a privileged male domain, a pattern that was linked to mainstream sport practices as well. (15).

The point here is that the particular activities into which students were directed did not simply *reflect* real differences in student interests or capacities, but actively *produced* them. This is a foundational argument in sport studies more broadly, but takes particular shapes and has particular (genocidal) effects in the context of settler colonialism.

The residential schooling system illustrates many of the layers to and complexities of settler colonial violence *in practice*. These are not, in other words, only abstract systems enshrined in policy. Rather, the settler state and its many agents put these systems into practice in the lives of thousands upon thousands of Indigenous children, shaping their understandings of themselves, their loved ones, and their histories, Nations, and cultures. Moreover, though the example of residential schooling is now relatively well-known (though rarely interrogated with sufficient depth and nuance), it is but one of myriad institutions that work in analogous ways and towards similar ends. It is but one example, that is, of the logic of elimination at work in the still settling state.

Reconciling What?

In recent decades, settler states have begun to reckon with the most obvious genocidal policies and practices of their pasts. In Canada, for example, the Canadian government mandated the Royal Commission on Aboriginal Peoples of the early 1990s "to investigate and propose solutions to the challenges affecting the relationship between Aboriginal peoples (First Nations, Inuit, Métis Nation), the Canadian government and Canadian society as a whole." [see digital repository, "Report of the Royal Commission on Aboriginal Peoples"] More recently, the TRC specifically interrogated the histories of residential schooling. In Australia, the Council for Aboriginal Reconciliation was established by a parliamentary Act in 1991, and is now part of a broad tapestry of organizations and bodies that work towards "researching and documenting of wars and massacres, but also in recognising Aboriginal and Torres Strait Islander sovereignty, contributions, and resilience, and actively recognising redress and healing" [see digital repository, "Truth-telling"]. Bodies like the TRC have made numerous key policy and practice recommendations (Calls to Action, in the case of the TRC) over the years. Some of the connections to sport and recreation are evident in these calls: TRC Calls 87-91 address sport and recreation specifically, as Call 89 exemplifies:

> We call upon the federal government to amend the Physical Activity and Sport Act to support reconciliation by ensuring that policies to promote physical activity as a fundamental element of health and well-being, reduce barriers to sports participation, increase the pursuit of excellence in sport, and build capacity in the Canadian sport system, are inclusive of Aboriginal peoples. [see digital repository, "Sports and Reconciliation"]

While the work of such organizations and commissions is not to be underestimated, it is also important to recognize three key limitations to such processes. First, progress on even the simplest of recommendations like the TRC's Calls to Action has been, and continues to be, painstakingly slow. Second, as vital as they are, such processes often focus on reparations for *past* harms (like those of residential schooling in Canada or the "stolen generation" of mostly mixed-race white and Indigenous children sent to boarding schools in Australia) rather than on institutions, policies, and practices inflicting harm *in the present* (Robinson, 2016). Third, as Anderson and Denis (2004) argue, such inquiries themselves are part of nation-making projects, constructing both the settler state and their relationships with Indigenous peoples and Nations in ways that serve to limit the possibilities of radical reimagining of governance (and relations more generally) in settler colonial contexts. The Canadian government, for instance, determined the contours of the TRC, setting the frame for the conversation is made and makes possible. The settler state assumes its own legitimacy and right to exist and govern, so of course the work of the TRC has to align with that same logic.

Importantly, processes such as those described above not only fail to address settler colonialism as it lives and breathes in the present, but also relegate past injustices to a past somehow disconnected from both the present and the future. Mann suggests that parliamentary processes and formal apologies (such as then Canadian Prime Minister Stephen Harper's apology for the horrors of residential schooling in 2008) fail to fundamentally *address* these injustices; instead, they work towards *settling* these pasts, resetting time as if these past injustices have nothing to do with contemporary violences in and of the settler state. These decisions, then, "are supposed to represent a closure of the questions of the past, fixing a common present as the foundation for a common future in which responsibility is clearly distributed between 'us'" (Mann, 2020, 439). Audra Simpson puts it in stark terms:

> This is the political language game and largely state-driven performance art that attempts to move elements of history forward in order to 'move on' from the past, to transition out of one period of history into another, better one. This dramaturgical solution appears as macro (and philosophical) antidote to the so-called problems of the past – 'historical injustice', the error of bad moral judgement and action, before. (2017, pp. 23-24)

In other words, such processes neatly contain the violences of settler colonialism in the past and thus hide from view the ongoing genocidal effects, logics, and practices.

Let us return to Call to Action 89, described above. With the arguments about the limits of inquiries and reconciliatory processes in mind, we might interrogate a Call to Action such as this one, constructed, of course, from within a state-driven process that (re)shapes findings and recommendations in fundamental ways. Below, I re-cite this Call to Action, inserting critical prompts at various points:

> We call upon the federal government to amend the Physical Activity and Sport Act [in which it will continue to define the

> parameters of what "counts" as sport and physical activity] to support reconciliation [also defined in colonial terms – as inclusion] by ensuring that policies to promote physical activity [only *some* kinds of physical activity by only *some* people, often led by non-Indigenous people and organizations] as a fundamental element of health and well-being, reduce barriers to [again, colonial] sports participation, increase the pursuit of excellence in sport, and build capacity in the Canadian sport system [actively ignoring or erasing Indigenous capacity and capacity-building], are inclusive of Aboriginal peoples.

Even in processes ostensibly oriented towards the project of reconciliation, then, we see how the network of spider webs works towards its own reproduction, not least in the realm of sport and physical activity. This is not to suggest, however, that Indigenous peoples passively accept these processes, a point to which I return most squarely in Chapter 4.

To be clear, the critique I highlight above is not a critique of the vital work done by TRC Commissioners, nor is it intended to take away from the courage of the more than 6500 witnesses who shared their heartfelt testimony with the Commission. The point, here, is that all of those folks did this important work within a structure determined by the colonial government itself, one that, by definition, circumscribed the parameters of the inquiry to a significant extent. You might think, for example, of a scenario in which Indigenous peoples claim that the Canadian government has infringed upon their rights (e.g., to fish, hunt, or engage in ceremony). What is the recourse of these Indigenous peoples who may or may not recognize the authority of the Canadian nation-state to govern? It is to appeal to the *Canadian* legal system, one specifically built as part of the "new social order" referred to above. To complain about a web of settler colonialism, in other words, they are directed to *yet another web*. The point, simply, is that the system itself is rigged. So, even when you have good, important work being done by Indigenous peoples to document the travesties of settler colonialism, it is often taking place from within a system designed to protect and reproduce itself.

Normalizing Narratives

Chen illuminates the layers of violence that characterize settler colonialism and points to the importance of "narratives that normalize, justify, and legitimize settler belonging to the land" (2021, p. 745). Because of these narratives, the violences of settler colonialism are seen not as the consequences of particular political decisions and pieces of legislation, for example, but as the unfortunate outcomes that have accrued over time in the process of "modernization."

Let us spend some time interrogating these narratives of belonging. In short, this refers to any stories that construct the claims of the settler state (and settlers) to the lands they occupy as legitimate. "Such stories," McGuire-Adams writes, "spin a rationalized space in the minds of settler-colonial people in order for their existence on stolen territory to make sense to them" (2020, p. 2). Here, I refer to stories in the broadest sense: we might think here of stories told in the media, in history textbooks, in public policy, and in innumerable other spaces. Stories do more, that is, than simply convey information; they "bring worlds into being" (Dutta, 2018, p. 94).

In settler states, the world "brought into being" through dominant stories is one in which settler colonialism is a completed project. It is a world in which the "modern" and modernizing forces of colonizers "developed" lands ripe for such activity. In this narrative, those already living on these lands were uncivilized, failing to take full advantage of the bounty that the lands represented. This is the logic underlying claims of *terra nullius* outlined above. The claim is not that there are no humans on these lands, but that those humans living on these lands are "uncivilized" – they are not "developing" these lands as they should from within this worldview. In this story, colonizers gradually asserted their "superior" ideas and systems (e.g., of government, technology, etc.), developed both the lands and the systems supporting the lives of those on these lands, and did so with the best of intentions. This narrative is not only one of the past, when occupied lands were "settled," but lives on in the present, with settler states asserting their continued occupation of these lands as entirely and permanently settled and legitimate. Rather, they would dismiss altogether the idea that they "occupy" the lands; instead, they would suggest that they *are* the lands – this is Canada (for example), after all... all who live here are *Canadians*. Simultaneously, settler states continue to deny Indigenous claims to sovereignty and nationhood, even at the very same moments that they might hearken to "nation-to-nation" relationships with Indigenous peoples in these occupied territories.

Perhaps you are wondering what shapes these stories take. I invite you, reader, to conjure your own examples of stories told that legitimate settler claims of belonging to lands. This is a particularly important (and often difficult) task if you are a settler in a settler state. You may not have thought of these as stories at all; they are simply the medium in which you have been raised as you occupied these lands yourself. (That was certainly my experience growing up as a white settler on lands claimed by Canada.) What kinds of narratives of belonging circulate in popular culture, in national rituals, in government discourse? What about in the world of sport?

We might look to the past for examples of such stories. Abenaki scholar Christine O'Bonsawin (2021), for instance, writes compellingly about "the assertion of Canada's colonial self" on the international stage through sport from the late 19th to the early 21st centuries. O'Bonsawin considers four periods within this broad time frame to position "sport as a form of social organization that was (and remains) firmly rooted within the apparatus of the colonial power" (2021, p. 277). In the late 19th and early 20th centuries, in the very early days of Canada as a nation-state (and the concomitant regulation of Indigenous lives through legislation such as the *Indian Act*), colonial agents organized carefully orchestrated sporting performances to tell a particular tale of the "new" nation. For example, in 1876, George Beers organized an international tour of two lacrosse teams – one composed of white Canadian settlers, the other of Kanien'kehá:ka (Mohawk) athletes. Unsurprisingly, tour organizers went to some length to make a spectacle of the Kanien'kehá:ka team, dressing them "in red and white jerseys and knickers, blue caps, beadwork, feathers, and jewelry, which was in stark contrast to the conservative uniforms of the white gentleman amateurs" (O'Bonsawin, 2021, p. 277). Tours such as this were designed to construct a distinct Canadian identity, one that showcased Indigenous peoples as symbols of European conquest.

In the early-to-mid 20th century, by contrast, Indigenous peoples were largely absent from the Canadian sporting scene. This period of extraordinary growth and success of Canada's international sporting achievements (including the era of the birth and expansion of the modern Olympic movement) was in lockstep, historically, with the institutionalization of huge numbers of Indigenous youth in residential and industrial schools. In this way, Canada depicts itself on the international sporting stage at this time with the near absence of Indigenous athletes, not because there were no Indigenous athletes of that calibre but because of an underlying impetus to eliminate Indigenous peoples *as Indigenous peoples*. Meanwhile, Canada was still *performing* Indigeneity in these burgeoning spaces of cultural production, albeit in deeply problematic ways. At the 1936 Berlin Olympics, for instance, a Canadian dance contingent performed a number of pieces, "including an Indigenous legend titled *Mala* and an Inuit legend titled *Mon-Ka-Ta*" (O'Bonsawin, 2021, p. 287). Though these performances were successful as Olympic performances, O'Bonsawin reminds us to keep in mind that:

> the performances were scripted in highly problematic ways and contained deeply possessive messages. As Indigenous peoples were surviving colonial oppression and violence in Canada, imprisoned on the reserves and within the residential schools, settler Canadians travelled to Nazi Germany, freely entered into another political space of unimaginable tyranny, and ultimately mirrored their own caricatured representations of an oppressed peoples from their homelands. (2021, p. 287)

These performances, then, perfectly illustrate the kinds of normalizing narratives referred to above. They not only rely upon, but also serve to reproduce, the idea that Canada had the right to claim these lands and to use Indigenous peoples, or even caricatures thereof, to sell itself on the international stage. Importantly, this is not to suggest that Indigenous peoples simply acquiesced to such practices, a point to which I return in Chapters 3 and 4.

It is not difficult to identify these kinds of normalizing narratives in the past. But what of the present? Let us consider the example of an elite sporting event – perhaps a game in the Women's National Basketball Association (in the United States), a USports volleyball match at a Canadian University, or an Aussie rules football match in Sydney. Prior to the beginning of the athletic contest, what do thousands of spectators do? What are they called to do, often explicitly?

Before many such matches, spectators are expected to stand and respectfully listen to or sing along with the national anthem (sometimes more than one in the case of two teams from different nation-states). Again, perhaps you find yourself thinking "sure, that's just what happens at games, a way of honouring the country in which they are being played." While that may be true, the national anthem does much more than simply honour a country; it actively produces a sense of belonging in and to that same country; it constructs that country as legitimate and as one towards which we should feel attached (Laurendeau, 2023; Stewart, 2021). Moreover, the regularity with which this ritual unfolds at sporting events in particular tells us something important about how sport and nation-making processes are interwoven, a topic to which I return in Chapter 3.

Conclusion

At the outset of this chapter, I posed these broad questions: Where do we see settler colonialism? How does it work? What are the logics upon which it is built? I invite you to pause now and consider whether you are better able to answer them now that you have contemplated this chapter. The point is not that settler colonialism is easy to define or that it looks exactly the same in different contexts. Quite the opposite, in fact: it is characterized by "shape-shifting tactics" (Alfred & Corntassel, 2005) as it perpetually works towards the possession of occupied lands and the naturalization of that possession. Webs, that is, are always in the process of being rebuilt and reshaped in response to challenges, to frays in the webs, etc.

In the next two chapters, equipped with a more nuanced understanding of the contours of settler colonialism, we put sport at the center of our analyses, highlighting how sport is a site of historical and ongoing colonial violence (Chapter 3) and simultaneously a social space in which settler colonialism is refused and contested (Chapter 4). Though we will consider these different dimensions of the entanglements of sport and settler colonialism, it is vital to remember that they are not so neatly separated in the social world; often, the very same context reveals *both* the violences of settler colonialism and the refusals of Indigenous peoples to acquiesce to those same violences.

Discussion Questions

- How is settler colonialism different from colonialism? Why does this difference matter?
- In what sense is settler colonialism a *network* or *constellation* of systems?
- What is the "logic of elimination"?
- How does the example of funding for Indigenous sport illustrate the logic of elimination?
- How do we make sense of the fact that some residential school survivors remember their sport experiences in these institutions in positive terms?
- How did sport in residential schooling shape Indigenous youths' understandings of land and space?
- What are "normalizing narratives" and how do they contribute to the settler colonial project?

CHAPTER 3

Sport, Recreation, and Colonial Violence

Introduction

What does genocide mean to you? How does it unfold? Perhaps you think of something like the Holocaust, the horrific processes by which millions perished in the ghastliest of ways. This would be entirely understandable as these events have been, quite rightly, taught in history books and storied in myriad ways in television and film. Or perhaps what comes to mind is something like the Rwandan genocide in which hundreds of thousands of mostly Tutsi were killed by Hutu militia members over 100 days as part of a brutal civil war. It is easy to see these horrendous events *as genocide*; images of violent murders saturate our understandings of these (and other) well-known genocides. What is perhaps less familiar to many readers is seeing and understanding genocide unfolding in their own social worlds and through a variety of means.

In Chapter 2, I briefly considered sport in residential school settings as an example of colonial violence. My hope is that many readers now understand this as a relatively clear example of how settler colonialism works in practice. In Chapter 3, I consider colonial violence in settler states in more depth and with explicit attention to how the lives of all peoples living in occupied territories are shaped by settler colonialism, though in very different ways.

I have referred in Chapters 1 and 2 to genocidal logics and practices, but what does that mean? In the Canadian context, authors of the TRC's final report, for instance, refer to *cultural genocide,* defining it as follows:

> the destruction of those structures and practices that allow the group to continue as a group. States that engage in cultural genocide set out to destroy the political and social institutions of the targeted group. Land is seized, and populations are forcibly transferred and their movement is restricted. Languages are banned. Spiritual leaders are persecuted, spiritual practices are forbidden, and objects of spiritual value are confiscated and destroyed. And, most significantly to the issue at hand, families are disrupted to prevent the transmission of cultural values and identity from one generation to the next. [See digital repository, "Honouring the Truth, Reconciling for the Future"]

This is an important way of naming residential schools (in this specific instance) *as genocidal*. It is also, however, a somewhat unsatisfying way of articulating the effects of this violent institution. For one thing, the victim-centered approach of the TRC meant that the focus was on the victims and not on the perpetrators. It was and remains important to hold space for the testimonies of survivors – those whose voices have so often been silenced or dismissed in these conversations. Yet, as I have written elsewhere, "the structure of the testimonials at the TRC [puts] the focus on the trauma that was suffered, not on the people and systems that perpetrated the harm" (Laurendeau, 2023, p. 120; see also Robinson, 2016).

For another, government lawyers prevented the TRC commissioners from calling the residential school system a genocide without the modifier of "cultural." Commissioner Murray Sinclair is on the record on this matter: "I had written a section for the report in which I very clearly called it genocide, and then I submitted that to the legal team and [they said] 'we can't [say that] because we can't make a finding of culpability, and that's very clear.' So, we did the next best thing" (quoted in MacDonald, 2019, p. 106). Cultural genocide (the "next best" label), I argue here, is simply genocide *in slow motion*. Given that the intent of the residential school system was undeniably to attack Indigenous cultural practices, languages, and kinship networks, it was clearly an attack on Indigenous peoples *as Indigenous peoples*. It was, in other words, an effort to prevent "the group [from continuing] as a group." Moreover, as described in Chapter 2, the residential schooling system was but one of a network of institutions and practices working towards this end. It is but one web in the network of webs that constitute the new social order of settler colonialism (Woolford, 2015). Together, the aim of this network *was and remains* to attack Indigenous peoples' cultures, practices, and, especially, their claims to occupied lands. Generally, this happens not through armed attack, which is what makes it somewhat more challenging to see as genocide. But it is no less genocidal for being enshrined in policy and practice, for it happening at the tip of a pen rather than the blade of a machete (Strakosch, 2015). Genocide is genocide, whatever the speed and whatever the mechanisms.

In this chapter, I consider a number of examples from the world of sport and recreation that help flesh out the question of *how* the settler state works towards these genocidal aims. When I teach a course called "Sport, Recreation, and Settler Colonialism," many students start the course imagining that it will be about sport in the lives of Indigenous peoples. While this is an important dimension of this work, it provides an incomplete, and I would even suggest irresponsible, picture of how settler colonialism operates.

Settler colonialism is a fundamentally *relational* system of power and privilege. It confers privilege on some while wreaking havoc in the lives of others. Moreover, this is not an either/or; it is not simply that one is either privileged or marginalized under settler colonialism. Rather, settler colonialism structures all lives in occupied territories in complex and often contradictory ways. In other words, all of us who live in occupied territories are entangled with this genocidal project.

In light of this point about relationality, it is vital that we do not artificially separate the impacts of colonialism on Indigenous peoples from how settler lives are structured in and by the settler state. My approach in this chapter, then, will be to consider a number of examples (most unfolding on lands claimed by Canada) that illustrate how sport and settler colonialism are interwoven and connect the lives of those living under colonial rule with the lives of those constructed as belonging in the settler state.

"Canada's Game"

Considered by many to be "Canada's game," ice hockey is a key site of social and cultural production. It is played by hundreds of thousands of Canadian youth, occupies centre stage in mediated professional sport in Canada, and hockey results are widely celebrated (anticipated, mourned, etc.) in exchanges at schools, workplaces, and on social media. Moreover, success on the international stage is the stuff of legend in Canada. Many Canadians, for instance, can tell you where they were when Jarome Iginla passed the puck to Sidney Crosby who one-timed it to win the gold medal in men's hockey at the Vancouver Winter Olympics in 2010. (I was in my living room raucously cheering with my family even though I'm not much of a hockey fan.) Overall, as Norman, Petherick, and Albert note, "Canadians often tell themselves, without apology or sense of irony, that hockey is 'our game'—Canadians invented it and it belongs to us" (2022, p. 323). These authors go on to note, however, that "both the game and the nation are imaginary constructions... laden with power relations as they reflect not necessarily what is, but rather a *desire*" (p. 1). It is with this question of *desire* in mind that I invite you to engage with this section in which I briefly examine "hockey through settler colonialism" (Norman, Petherick, and Albert, 2022, p. 329). Whether or not you are familiar with or invested in hockey, I urge you to consider what kinds of desires the game and its place in the Canadian popular imaginary reveal. What does the game have to tell us about who Canadians imagine themselves to be, about the kinds of belonging Canadians wish for?

Given the importance of hockey in Canadian popular culture, it is instructive to think a bit more deeply about what *kinds* of cultural ideas circulate in and around the game. As Mary Louise Adams writes in an oft-quoted piece, "if hockey is life in Canada, then life in Canada remains decidedly masculine and white" (2006, p. 71). Adams elaborates: "Hockey produces a very ordinary but pernicious sense of male entitlement: to space, to status, to national belonging" (2006, p. 71). More recent research reinforces Adams' point, highlighting that it is not just men, but *white* men in particular imagined as in and of both hockey spaces and the nation (Adams, 2014; Kennedy et. al., 2019; Norman et. al., 2022). In other words, to the extent that Canadians imagine hockey as "our game," it is telling *who* is imagined as part of that story and in what ways. All of this points to the importance of hockey as a "site of Canadian nation-making, where ongoing embodied acts of settler occupation in the game serve to naturalize settler belonging on, and entitlement to, the land" (Norman, Petherick, & Albert, 2022, p. 223).

Consider the case of the recently disbanded Beardy's Blackhawks. As youth sport becomes ever more governed by strictly rational logics of economics and player development (think here of the proliferation of high-performance hockey schools), leagues like the Saskatchewan Hockey Association (SHA) continually reflect on their organizational structures. In that context, the case of the Beardy's team is an important one indeed, as this team represented "Canada's only U18 AAA hockey franchise located on and operated by a First Nation" before it was disbanded at the end of the 2019/2020 season (McKegney et. al., 2021, p. 32). Recent research points to the value of this team as a space for both Indigenous and non-Indigenous players. Indigenous players had a rare opportunity to be part of an organized sporting space managed by Indigenous peoples and with Indigenous ways of knowing and being valued and supported; the team "offered an elite hockey space in which Indigenous players could bring their full selves into the dressing room" (McKegney et. al., 2021, p. 32). Moreover, as Norman, Petherick and Albert's research demonstrates, teams rooted in Indigenous communities give some Indigenous youth the chance to embody the "sovereignty that comes with playing for Nation, with kin, on ancestral lands" (2022, p. 226). Non-Indigenous players, meanwhile, had the opportunity to share time and space with Indigenous peoples on and off the ice, helping to break down the misconceptions and a lack of knowledge so endemic in non-Indigenous Canada.

Despite the benefits outlined above, the SHA decided to disband the team, pointing to the idea that the "unique characteristics of the Beardy's Blackhawks are no longer needed in contemporary Saskatchewan" (McKegney et. al., 2021 p. 44). With these words, the league General Manager draws on a post-racial imagination of a Canada (and league) in which barriers to full participation have been meaningfully addressed, relieving both the country and the league of the obligation to do the hard work of (re)considering their own complicity in ongoing racialized violence (McKegney et. al., 2021). This too-easy framing denies the very real differences and complexities that resonates in the lives of (potential) Indigenous players in the league and undercuts the value of Indigenous-led and organized spaces not only for Indigenous players but also for those non-Indigenous players on such teams, and, indeed, for settler-community teams who might travel there to play (more on that below).

One telling dimension of the research with this team relates to what happened on the ice when the Beardy's teams would play against other (non-Indigenous) teams in the league. Routinely, Beardy's players would be met with racism from both their opponents and fans in the stands. This is important in a number of respects. First, the fact that even non-Indigenous players on the Beardy's team experienced this racism (with helmets and faceguards on, they would be seen as Indigenous simply because of their membership on this team) means that these players and their loved ones came to understand at a deeper level the extent to which their Indigenous teammates experienced this kind of racism in the league and in their lives more generally; playing on the team afforded them "opportunities to witness, experience, and, at times, address racism that are seldom available to non-racialized Canadians" (McKegney et. al., 2021, p. 32). Second, researchers highlight that these kinds of micro-aggressions are so pervasive that Indigenous players (and parents) often shrug them off as simply the way things are, a phenomenon McKegney et. al. dub "manufactured compliance." Third, the particular shapes that these micro-aggressions take are quite telling. Specifically, opponents would tell Beardy's players to "go back" to the reserve, to teepees, or other such tropes of Indigeneity. McKegney and colleagues argue that:

> The cadence "go back" ... works to register the unbelonging of racialized players in hockey spaces, marking the coloured body

> as out of place. For Black athletes and athletes of colour, the racist taunt "go back"—much like its more covert manifestation in the microaggression, "where are you from, really?"—works to police white entitlement by constructing white settlers as authentic Canadians while implying non-whites belong elsewhere. (2021, p. 38)

This points to critically important ideas about belonging and at-homeness on lands claimed by the settler state. It highlights the sense in which these opponents (and, by extension, settlers in Canada more generally) understand "the reserve" (in an abstract sense) as the place where Indigenous peoples "belong," and simultaneously produces white settlers' entitlement to occupied territories.

Lest we think that this is simply a phenomenon on the ice (playing field, etc.), it is vital to note that similar discourses are pervasive in current media and political discussions of so-called "homeless encampments" in Canadian cities. Indigenous peoples are disproportionately represented among the unhoused in many cities (including my "home" city of Lethbridge, for example). Many municipal governments (and much of the citizenry they represent) are deeply concerned about these "encampments," but popular discourse suggests that their concern is largely for the "blight" these encampments supposedly represent – the sense in which they make others (settlers) in the city feel unsafe. Moreover, in keeping with neoliberal framings of social problems, those who face barriers to housing are understood not as citizens deserving of support from the community and state, but as individuals who have simply "failed" to meet their basic personal needs. Their efforts to create and sustain shelter are treated as dangers to themselves and their communities, their presence treated as a nuisance, and their worldly possessions seen as "biohazards" that need to be "cleaned up" for the good of the community. (The irony of phrases like "compassionate clean-up" in such discussions is lost, it seems, on most municipal political leaders – see Belanger & Laurendeau, 2022.) Much of the public discourse around this question returns to the idea that urban Indigenous peoples should "go back home" to get the support that they might need or want. That all of this unfolds on lands of spiritual and cultural importance to these very people, lands stolen from them through a constellation of colonial policies and practices, rarely merits mention.

Another example from minor hockey serves to illustrate the entanglement of the cultural politics of hockey and the settler colonial project. Norman, Petherick, and Albert (2022) consider a telling shift in the structure of the Keystone Junior Hockey League (KJHL) in the province of Manitoba. Five teams from non-Indigenous communities elected to leave the KJHL and form a separate league. Their departure left only five teams, all from Indigenous communities, in the KJHL. Though the departing teams pointed to economics and traffic safety as rationalizations for the move, Norman and colleagues point out the weaknesses of the claims. The non-Indigenous teams did not consult with the Indigenous teams before leaving, and some of the remaining KJHL teams were located near the teams that formed the new league. Norman and colleagues argue that "this split is not a trivial quibble over league boundaries, but is reflective of the ongoing struggle to fortify White settler belonging, a belonging that is undermined by sovereign First Nations teams playing 'Canada's game' in the KJHL" (p. 225).

Norman, Petherick, and Albert further suggest that the teams with direct connections to First Nations exemplify Indigenous sovereignties on multiple levels and that such sovereignties were seen as threats to settler belonging among the teams based in settler communities, thus pointing to the more important rationale for these teams' departure. They situate the departure of these five teams to form a new league, then, as one of the "shape-shifting practices" of the present that illustrate the ongoing "history of disciplining peoples through the reserve system and sport" (2022, p. 228). Their analysis highlights "the lived, embodied and relational materiality of Indigenous sovereignties [exemplified by the teams in Indigenous communities] that are incommensurable with, and thus irreducible to, settler sovereignty" (p. 226). It is this incommensurability, they suggest, that ultimately motivated the five teams to leave. Moreover, whatever the motivation, such a move and rationalization reproduces two key ideas. First, it reinforces the notion that "the reserve" is a place of danger, one from which (settler) youth should be protected. Second, the rationale from league organizers defends the myth that Canada (and hockey) are not racist spaces. Indigenous players are still welcome, the argument goes, so clearly "we" are not racist. As Norman and colleagues note, however, the underlying logics are carefully buttressed by appeals to "safety" and economics, meaning, ultimately, that Indigenous *players* are welcome on (non-Indigenous teams) so long as they adhere to the colonial logics of the (new) league. "We" welcome Indigenous players, that is, so long as they embody "our" team spirit etc.; so long as their presence doesn't undermine "our" claiming of lands and belonging.

Lacrosse

Lacrosse is perhaps the clearest example of the complexities, nuances, and contradictions of sport and settler colonialism. As noted in Chapter 2, lacrosse has been marshalled by settler Canada as part of storying the nation on an international stage. Here, I delve deeper into the history of the activity, how settlers colonized the game and claimed it as their own as part of a project of claiming the lands themselves. However, I also point towards how Indigenous Nations and organizations have used lacrosse to resist and refuse colonial rule, ideas that I develop more fully in Chapter 4. Taken together, these dimensions of the histories of lacrosse illuminate the tensions, contradictions, and contestedness of settler colonialism.

As Downey notes, "lacrosse has been a central element of Indigenous cultures and worldviews for centuries" (2018, p. 38). There is ample evidence that the game has long been played on lands now claimed by Canada and the United States, and that it took slightly different forms (e.g., the number, size, and particular shapes of the balls and sticks) depending on the particular context in which the game was played. In Indigenous worldviews, lacrosse was never, however, simply a game. Rather, playing lacrosse was often a way of practicing spirituality and culture, a form of dispute resolution, and a way of knowing. It stands to reason, then, that the stick itself "was, and continues to be, more than just a piece of sports equipment; rather, it is alive and is a form of medicine that allows the game to heal, whether an individual, a community, or a nation" (Downey, 2018, p. 38).

As colonial powers began to assert themselves on Indigenous lands in what is now known as North America, lacrosse continued to be an important practice in Indigenous Nations. Ironically, it was not initially targeted by colonial agents even though the latter thought the game uncivilized, as they failed to appreciate the deeper meaning of the game for Indigenous peoples (Downey, 2018). However, in "the mid-nineteenth century, when settlers were in the process of creating a Canadian identity, the relationship between Indigenous Nations and lacrosse began to shift dramatically as non-Natives increasingly participated in the game and appropriated it as their own" (Downey, 2018, pp. 42-43). As Canadian confederation (1867) approached, British immigrants in Montreal, in particular, took up the activity, codified a set of rules, introduced non-Indigenous governing bodies, and declared the game the national sport of the "new" nation (Downey, 2018). Montreal dentist Dr. William George Beers was a member of the Montreal Lacrosse Club (MLC) and is generally considered a key figure in colonizing the game, having been largely responsible for crafting a uniform set of rules, thus standardizing the parameters of such contests (Downey, 2018). As discussed in Chapter 2, he organized the lacrosse tour that asserted "Canada's colonial" self on the world stage. The standardization of rules also undercut the *relationality* embedded in the previously accepted practice among Indigenous peoples of negotiating the contours of the games prior to each contest (Downey, 2018). Downey describes the overall effect:

> By standardizing the rules, Beers helped to colonize a particular version of the game, that of the Kanien'kehá:ka, transforming it into the "authentic" variant. Field sizes were significantly shortened, and strict rules were implemented to counter Indigenous expectations of physicality and to curb the supposedly violent racialized aspects of the game to make it more widely appealing to Canadians. (p. 44)

Overall, this served to cast "the game in classic colonial dichotomies: it was allegedly the uncivilized pursuit of a disappearing people, but it could be salvaged if it were infused with Western ideas about sportsmanship, athleticism, and scientific regulation" (Downey, 2018, p. 43).

"Salvaging" the game involved first limiting, and later prohibiting altogether, the participation of Indigenous players in organized lacrosse. These processes, unfolding in the late 19th and early 20th centuries, were part of the project of both constructing and disseminating a distinctively Canadian (sporting) identity, one "connected to the land they now occupied" (Downey, 2018, p. 43). This is not to suggest, however, that Indigenous peoples stopped playing the game; rather, they creatively adapted to the shifting circumstances amidst the various pressures of colonial invasion:

> as anglophone settlers increasingly employed the game in nation-building activities such as holiday celebrations, and encouraged immigration through oversees lacrosse tours, Indigenous peoples used their cultural identities, both 'authentic' and 'fabricated,' to secure additional income, fame, and the opportunity to travel. (Downey, 2018, pp. 43-44; also see O'Bonsawin, 2021)

This was a time of tremendous upheaval for Indigenous peoples and Nations, and we must keep in view their forms of overt and covert resistance to the emerging colonial order and, simultaneously, recognize these "sporting experiences as firmly rooted within the apparatus of colonial power" (O'Bonsawin, 2021, p. 280).

The newly standardized game of lacrosse took hold in other urban centres in Canada, becoming part of a process of constructing a national (sporting) identity rooted in colonial and middle-class Victorian sensibilities It came to embody the values of "respectability," "self-discipline," and hard work, all defined, of course, in colonial terms. Writing of both lacrosse and snowshoeing, Gilliant Poulter suggests that "[e]ngaging in these activities was a way to demonstrate the civility, autonomy and distinctiveness of the nation's subjects, and a practice which might develop a popular consensus regarding national identity" (2003, p. 314). Lacrosse also spread globally, becoming a major international sport, the cornerstone of which was the version of the game largely appropriated and codified by Beers (Downey, 2018).

The internationalization of the game was, and remains, important in terms tethered to settler colonial processes or nation-making. For most of the 20th century, for instance, Indigenous teams were excluded from international competition, not least because organizational bodies such as the International Lacrosse Federation (ILF) did not recognize them as representing sovereign Nations. In other words, even though the game's roots arose from Indigenous lands and Nations, those same Nations were not recognized *as nations* for the purposes of international competition. Moreover, when Indigenous representatives lobbied various bodies for such recognition, settler states generally opposed their efforts. For example, when the Haudenosaunee Nationals (then called the Iroquois Nationals) petitioned for acceptance in the ILF in the 1980s, the most significant resistance came from Canadian and Australian representatives of the ILF. As Downey explains: "The Canadians, who were most opposed, feared that acceptance could set a precedent and that the ILF might have to accommodate other Indigenous nations… Like the Canadians, the Australians feared setting a precedent with respect to sovereignty and Indigenous athletes in their own country" (Downey, 2018, p. 214). The two settler states, then, were concerned that recognizing the sovereignty of Haudenosaunee peoples would both set a precedent politically and "drain the talent pool" of the Canadian and Australian nations (recall that from a colonial mindset, a Haudenosaunee athlete is a *Canadian* athlete). In essence, they feared that "if we recognize their sovereignty, we'll have to recognize their sovereignty!"

Lacrosse is one of Canada's official sports, said to represent what Canada is and Canadians do. Lacrosse *does* represent Canada in some important ways, though not in ways Canada's sport leaders might have us believe. Rather, it is arguably the most Canadian of sports in that colonists stole it from Indigenous peoples, changed the rules to make it more "civilized," actively worked to prevent Indigenous peoples from playing it both on their homelands and in international competition, and claimed it as emblematic of the emerging nation. It is vital to note, however, how Indigenous peoples have resisted, refused, and creatively negotiated colonial rule in and through lacrosse. I consider this reality in greater depth in Chapter 4.

Outdoor Recreation

I invite you to consider the example of outdoor recreation – activities such as hiking, rock climbing, backcountry camping, etc. As we embark on this discussion, I encourage you to think about your own relationships with these activities. Do you like to "head to the mountains" as an escape from city life, to recharge from the stresses of work and/or school, for example? Do you see practitioners of these activities represented in magazines, on social media or film, or in the (virtual) pages of outdoor stores like Mountain Equipment Company (Canada) or Recreational Equipment Inc. (U.S.)?

For many of us in settler states, the idea of the "natural beauty" of our home countries is one that is deeply familiar. I grew up in Canada, the so-called "great white north." In the Canadian context, places like Banff National Park are more than simply sought-after tourist destinations. They are part of how the nation is built, both geographically and metaphorically. Geographically, many of these park spaces were among the lands claimed and "developed" as the settler state took shape. Metaphorically, however,

Author and friend canoeing on the Bow River in Banff National Park.

they were and are part of how the nation is *storied*, how it is sold as an idea. The park now known as Banff National Park was marketed as part of the project of drawing European settlers to Western Canada, for instance (Laurendeau, 2020; Mason, 2014). Moreover, these spaces continue to be part of how Canada tells stories about itself on both national and international stages. These "wild spaces" are part of the story of Canada, part of how we sell ourselves as a beautiful and desirable place to live or visit.

However, there are more layers to this storying than simply beautiful places. There are also stories being produced about who belongs in these beautiful places and to whom these places belong. In order to more fully understand this idea, we need to consider the idea of wilderness itself.

Though wilderness is often thought of as simply a descriptor of something that exists in the world around us ("nature" works in very similar ways), the production of the idea of the wilderness is, in fact, one central to the settler colonial project (Laurendeau, 2020; Laurendeau, Higham & Peers, 2021; Vander Kloet, 2009). Settler colonists in Canada and the U.S., for instance, engaged in sustained political projects as they created and "protected" these park spaces (Spence, 1999). In order for them to be understood as "wild" (and thus as desirable spaces to visit), these spaces first needed to be cleared of the people who were already there living in deep relation with the lands themselves. The creation of many national parks, then, *must* be understood as part of the broader project of land dispossession in which settler states like Canada engaged (and engage – more on that below).

As Adams notes, "Sporting spaces... are constitutive of and constituted by particular bodies, by how certain bodies are invited into that space, and by the actions and movements of these bodies" (2014, p. 203). In the case of revered outdoor spaces, we must ask ourselves which bodies are invited into these spaces, which are imagined to be "at home" in these spaces, and which bodies are considered "out of place." The question, in other words, is of which bodies are imagined as constitutive of particular spaces and places, of "how particular bodies are positioned as of and in a space, while at the same time not quite belonging to it" (Puwar, 2004, p. 8). More pointedly, Puwar argues that "social spaces are not blank and open for any body to occupy... Some bodies are deemed as having the right to belong, while others are... in accordance with how spaces and bodies are imagined (politically, historically, and conceptually), circumscribed as being 'out of place'" (p. 8).

What all of this suggests is that outdoor recreation activities and the representation thereof are connected to both histories of land dispossession and ideas about entitlements to the use of (and profit from) these beautiful landscapes. They are part, that is, of how the nation is storied and re-storied over time (e.g., Wigglesworth, 2021).

Even in the present where we see some meaningful initiatives towards better acknowledging Indigenous historical presence on lands such as these, we see processes of settler myth-making unfold. In Waterton Lakes National Park in Southern Alberta, for example, park officials have collaborated with local First Nations to some extent on park initiatives. Recent and ongoing changes to signage do much more to educate visitors about Blackfoot presence on these lands, Blackfoot terms for mountains, flora and fauna, even Blackfoot ceremony and spirituality [see digital repository, "Waterton Lakes Visitor Centre"]. These are welcome and consequential changes that stand to help visitors better understand the histories of the lands and the park itself. What they fall short of, however, is highlighting the *dispossession* of the lands or any imperative to return lands to those who have been there since time immemorial. In that sense, the park is *still* engaged in the process of national myth-making; the myth now, though, is of a benevolent nation better recognizing what are seen as past oversights. This works to acknowledge these histories but simultaneously to circumscribe them. The story now being told, in other words, is of a park (and a country) committed to more fully *including* Indigenous peoples, histories, languages, etc. But this is only one story that might be told. Imagine, if you will, a story that goes rather differently: "This is a park built on, and inescapably tied to, lands stolen through multiple processes of colonial violence, and the only way to make that right is by giving up colonial control over the lands themselves." I suggest that for many settlers this is an unthinkable story – one that does not align with how they understand themselves and their country. But that is part of the point… through the kinds of relationship to these lands enshrined in policy, in institutional practice, in educational curricula and more, the settler state renders certain ways of storying the country – of storying the injustices upon which the country is built – unthinkable. This is one of the effects of the *webs*. Not only do they trap Indigenous peoples, but they limit and circumscribe the ideas in circulation, ideas that might make different kinds of social organization imaginable. The "normalizing narratives" referred to in Chapter 2, in other words, are parts of the webs themselves.

A Colonial Logic of Containment

Norman, Hart, and Petherick theorize that ongoing settler colonial rule "operates through discursive and nondiscursive practices of fixing and arresting the dynamic and ongoing movement of cultures, ideas, and bodies within a colonial logic of containment"

(2019, p. 120). In other words, for settler colonial assumed authority to (continue to) govern to be maintained, limits of various kinds must be placed on the movement and circulation of actual Indigenous peoples. Moreover, limitations must also extend to practices (i.e., the ban on the Sundance and other ceremonies), language (i.e., prohibitions on those who attended residential school from speaking their home languages), and, indeed, ideas about Indigenous peoples, which proliferate in sports. I elaborate on some of these dimensions below.

Let us return to the question of residential schooling system, both to further flesh out the contours of its violences and to illustrate the sense in which residential schooling is not a thing of the past but echoes in contemporary policy and practice through shared logics.

Norman, Hart, and Petherick build on Forsyth's vital work on the place of sport in residential schools in their interrogation of the colonial logics of containment. They highlight that the activities and organizational strategies Forsyth describes – e.g., spatially defined playing fields, military drills – worked to limit Indigenous peoples' movements. They worked, in other words, to shape the ways children in these institutions understood themselves, their bodies, and their relationship to space itself. Norman and colleagues argue that this is foundational to the colonial project: "The control of movement is central to the process of colonization" (Norman et. al., 2019, p. 113).

Norman, Hart, and Petherick also highlight the sense in which the organization of sport in residential schools is part of the "biopolitics of heteropatriarchal normativities" (Norman et. al., 2019, p. 115). This is theoretically dense idea, one worth teasing apart in some detail. Biopolitics is the management and regulation of people at the macro level; the management of bodies and the population through indirect, rather than direct, rule (you might think here of food guides, for instance). Heteropatriarchy is a social organization in which (cis)heterosexual men are privileged in terms of kinship systems, law, politics, etc. Taken together, these terms describe a system in which heterosexual relations and the "rule of the father" are constructed as normative in the service of managing (containing) people at the population level. The point is that sport in residential schools worked to interrupt not only particular Indigenous relations (e.g., by separating children from their parents and siblings from each other), but Indigenous kinship systems in general through the production and valorization of patriarchal gender relations through the gendered division of activities, for instance.

The logic of containment is evident, too, they argue, at the levels of policy and representation. At a policy level, the settler state continues to govern and fund sport according to settler logics. As noted in Chapter 2, this involves providing funding for initiatives and sports that adhere to colonial logics. Even in the context of so-called "reconciliation," this continues to produce a paternalistic relationship between the settler state and Indigenous peoples, operating according to a "we (the settler state) know best" ethos. As just one example, in the wake of the TRC final report, the Canadian federal government's 2018 budget allocated nearly $50 million towards Indigenous sport and social development, responding to the TRC Calls to Action that called for more "inclusive" funding models for sport and recreation. The fundamental problem, however, is that these dollars largely flowed not to existing Indigenous organizations but to a non-Indigenous organization, called Right to Play (RTP), whose purpose is to foster sport for social development internationally. This framework upholds the logic of elimination.

This funding model has real, material consequences in the sense that well-established Indigenous organizations such as the

Aboriginal Sport Circle (ASC) do not receive adequate funding. Better funding organizations like the ASC would support the development of much-needed capacity in, for, and with Indigenous Nations. The colonial funding model also means significant flows of resources to non-Indigenous international organizations like RTP, organizations simply not equipped to provide culturally sensitive and informed programming. Instead, such organizations build "neutral resources" meant to be marshalled in many international contexts (Essa et. al., 2022, p. 302). Arellano and Downey argue that these "allegedly 'apolitical and universal' sport for development initiatives" often exemplify "shape-shifting" colonial interventions and serve to undercut the ability of Indigenous Nations and Indigenous-led organizations to engage in capacity-building and culturally relevant and sensitive programming (2019, p. 471). Furthermore, such a funding model becomes yet another way in which "power imbalances are entrenched, positioning settler sport organizations as the authority on Indigenous sport, physical culture and social development" (Norman et. al., 2019, p. 118). Finally, it reproduces the powerful idea that Indigenous peoples and organizations are fundamentally "broken" and that the solution to any challenges before them is social development "support" from colonial bodies, once again reasserting colonial authority (Tuck, 2009).

Policy also works according to a colonial logic in the sense that those physical activities considered for funding initiatives are evaluated against the implicit model of colonial sport. In processes such as this, Indigenous sport and physical cultural practices are produced as "exotic," frozen in time, and their dynamism and evolution in contemporary Indigenous communities and lives are erased. In valorizing particular "authentic" forms of Indigenous sport, games, and physical activity, such as the finger pull, high kick, or knuckle hop, the settler state perpetuates understandings of Indigeneity and Indigenous peoples "as 'stuck' in the past, unchanging, and thus tragically dying in the face of unyielding processes of modernization" (Norman et. al., 2019, p. 119). Heine (2014) argues that activities such as these are marshalled as "museum pieces" and thus also divorced from the spiritual and cultural roots of the activities, many of which work directly to foster connections between Indigenous peoples and their homelands (Paraschak and Heine, 2019). Recall here the point from Chapter 2 about "normalizing narratives." One such narrative is, quite simply, that Indigenous peoples no longer exist – or at least that they no longer exist *as Indigenous peoples.* Indigenous peoples, in this narrative, have been largely absorbed into the Canadian body politic, and as such they have no special claim to nationhood, sovereignty, or reparations for what are understood to be past harms. This is one of the ways in which we see the "violent self-justification through the erasure of Indigenous peoples as anything but an empty symbol" (Justice, 2018, p. 10), referred to in Chapter 2.

Justice's notion of the reduction of Indigenous peoples to "an empty symbol" is a vital one. It is worth some additional unpacking, however, to better understand *how* this symbolism becomes part of a "violent self-justification." As noted above, to the extent that settler state policies and practice erase or deny the contemporary realities, politics, strengths, and claims of Indigenous peoples, this justifies the ongoing entrenchment of deeply unequal political relationships between state agents and Indigenous peoples in occupied territories. But there is more to the story.

The (attempted) reduction of Indigenous peoples to the realm of the symbolic is about producing ideas of Indigeneity, but it is also always about producing ideas about (good) settlers. The policy example above, for instance, not only perpetuates damaging ideas about Indigenous people's supposed inability to govern and organize themselves and their own sporting activities, but simultaneously (re)creates the idea that settler organizations and the settler state are and should be the "saviours" of Indigenous peoples. By positioning settler organizations and political bodies as those responsible for "social development," policies such as this position settlers as the experts, as helpful and benevolent agents somehow working towards reconciliation. At one and the same time, then, such policies and processes story Indigenous peoples, the settler state, and the country itself in ways that freeze Indigenous peoples in time and erase their complexity in the present, while producing settlers and settler organizations as agents of positive change (Norman et. al., 2019).

To further develop this point, let us return to the idea of Indigenous mascotry. The reduction of Indigenous peoples to the symbolic works as a foil against which (particular) settlers can understand themselves. Norman et. al. theorize that Indigenous mascotry appeared in North American sport culture curing a so-called "crisis of masculinity" – a moment in the early twentieth century characterized by worry about a "softening of culture and the associated feminization of white boys and men" (Norman et. al., 2019, p. 119). In this context, they argue, white settler youth – boys especially – engaged in various practices of "playing Indian," of drawing on imagined hypermasculine Indigeneity, as they constructed their own masculine identities. This process was not confined to youth, nor was it limited to boys and men specifically, as these same tropes were commodified and marketed to fans of elite sport:

> Here, the spectacle of the heroic battle-hardened brave or the stoic chief captured in the sporting mascot would exhilarate consuming fans as they appropriated the status of these once proud, but now defeated (or so the rhetoric goes), warriors as a method of shoring

> up the embodied contours of white, masculine, settler colonial subjectivities. (Norman et. al., 2019, p. 119)

Again, this illustrates the relationality of settler colonialism. At one and the same time, these tropes construct a narrow image of Indigeneity *and* become key elements of the constitution of how settlers understand themselves. The image of the "battle-hardened brave" refuses and erases the complexities in the lives of Indigenous peoples. It becomes one of the tropes of Indigeneity too often drawn on in broader social and political discussions, such as when United States Supreme Court Justice Samuel Alito suggested that before Europeans arrived, "tribes were at war with each another," as if that is all we need know about pre-colonial history on these lands [see digital repository, "Conservative Supreme Court Justices Question"]. That this should come from a justice of the "highest court of the land" is unsurprising in light of how widely (and seemingly innocently) this idea circulates in many cultural arenas, including that of elite sport.

Even defenses of Indigenous mascotry become part of the construction of tropes of Indigeneity. Often, teams with such names and/or mascots argue that they are "honouring" Indigenous peoples and/or that local Indigenous peoples or Nations support their use. The former is, quite simply, laughable – it should be evident by now that such mascots do nothing to *honour* Indigenous peoples, working instead to circulate problematic and stereotypical ideas and images about Indigenous peoples. The latter rationale is a more thorny one, as Indigenous support or consent is important and often overlooked. However, suggesting that Indigenous mascotry is not harmful because *some* Indigenous peoples support it flattens the complexities of Indigenous people and cultures. This line of argument allows for a small number of Indigenous voices to stand in for all Indigenous peoples; again, it erases the complexities of Indigenous peoples and political positions. It is possible for some Indigenous peoples to be agents of colonial oppression, just as it is possible for some racialized peoples to be complicit in the reproduction of systemic racism. Denying these complexities and contradictions becomes yet another way in which tropes of Indigeneity are (re)produced.

In a later piece, Norman, Petherick, and Albert elaborate how the colonial logic of containment is evident in the context of youth hockey that involves teams based on reserves. I discussed this work looking at the reorganization of the KJHL above; here, I quote them at length to illustrate the layers of colonial violence in operation in this example:

> The logics of containment function at multiple levels including geographically, legally, and discursively (see also Coulthard, 2014). Indeed, we can see all three of these dimensions playing out in the contemporary moment when it comes to the reserve, sport, and recreation. For example, the fact that many reserves are situated in geographically remote locations, along with the discursive construction of reserves as spaces of violence and hostility (Moreton-Robinson, 2015), together mark the reserve as an undesirable place for settler athletes to travel to for competition (see Robidoux, 2004). In too many cases, this has effectively resulted in what Robidoux (2004) refers to as the "ghettoization" of Indigenous athletics. This ghettoization materializes informally, to be sure, through interpersonal racism, but also through a number of overlapping legislative practices, including the outright exclusion of First Nations teams from league play (see McKegney et al., 2019; Robidoux, 2004), the reorganization of leagues along racial lines, ... or through mandating that First Nations teams and athletes located in remote locations must travel long distances to more urban centers to compete in league play, where settler

teams do not make the trip to reserves (Skerritt & Giroday, 2012). No matter what the containment strategy, the outcome is all too familiar, as reserves are continuously disciplined by a settler logic that includes the dual practices of exclusion and assimilation. (2022, p. 328)

Norman and colleagues emphasize, though, that "the reserve" is more than simply a space of containment (physically and discursively). Though it is a key site of colonial violence enshrined in policy and practice, it is also, they argue, "a complex social, cultural, and spiritual place that has, in many cases, served as a site of Indigenous survivance and resistance" (2022, p. 330). This is a point to which I return in Chapter 4.

All of this, Norman and colleagues suggest, exemplifies the logic of containment described above: "displacing, spatially confining, and restricting mobilities are pivotal strategies by which European settlers have dispossessed Indigenous peoples of their land and sought to destroy the ability of the 'group to continue as a group'" (2019, p. 113).

Pedagogies of Settler Subjectivity

One of the clearest ways in which the settler state (not least the world of sport therein) shapes the lives of settlers is by teaching them a sense of entitlement to occupy the lands on which they live, work, and play. Recall that the *webs* both constrain the lives of Indigenous peoples *and* support settlers in occupied territories. This sense of entitlement is produced through encounters with what I call "pedagogies of settler subjectivity." Pedagogies refer to the ways of learning and knowing, and are among the normalizing narratives referred to in Chapter 2. The point here is that "settlers become settlers. We are always… settlers in-the-making, and we are being (re)made as such through quotidian encounters" such as those that unfold in numerous sporting contexts (Laurendeau, p. 99; also see Chen, 2021). Recall the point from Chapter 1 that being a settler is not (simply) about what is in our DNA, who our ancestors were or when they arrived in occupied territories. Rather, it is about our location in a network of systems of power and privilege, our location in the network of webs. Key to this location are ways of understanding the location itself to be *just* and something to which settlers are entitled. As such, settlers must learn (and relearn, and relearn) the "correctness" of our location, the idea that we *belong* here. This is what we learn through pedagogies of settler subjectivity, including those we encounter in and through sport.

Consider what happens at an elite sporting event, for instance. Attending games of the National Hockey League's Calgary Flames as a child, I routinely encountered numerous pedagogies that taught me my place in the social world and, indeed, the contours of that world itself. Attending these games with my dad, I was taught that I lived in a place called Calgary, unquestionably part of a country called Canada, one to be honoured by standing at attention with my hat removed for the singing of the national anthem prior to the game. I learned, too, that it was perfectly acceptable for Indigenous peoples to be seen as caricatures – as mascots for a number of the teams that visited the Saddledome (and, importantly, for several of the schools in the city that were rivals in sporting events of various kinds).

The anthem, however, does much more than simply "honour" a country, as I pointed out in Chapter 2. At a deeper level, it produces a sense of belonging in and loyalty to that country. It produces, in other words, the idea that those hailed to stand and sing (or at least respectfully listen) are entitled, as members of the

Sport, Recreation, and Colonial Violence

nation, to occupy these lands and call them "Canada" (in this instance). At sporting events (and elsewhere), national anthems are more than simply part of the pre-game ritual; they do important work in producing both feelings and ideas. As McDonald notes, "the imagining of the nation works through the concealment of this constant process of ritualized repetition of symbols and ceremonies—including that of the ritual of singing the anthem—as constitutive of the nation" (2020, p. 4). On this point, it is worth recalling the idea that spider webs are difficult to see from certain angles. The national anthem, for instance, is seen by many as simply a moment of patriotism, not as an explicit mechanism of (racialized) nation-building.

In a sustained interrogation of the Canadian national anthem, Stewart analyzes the hailing referred to above:

> "O Canada" seeks to bring into being the existence of Canada as a dominant ideological concept, by both asserting itself as a nation and asserting its subjects as its possessions, declaring that Canada is "native land" that "all of us" must "stand on guard for." The anthem ...hails "all of us" into being as subjects of the nation, as long as "we" identify with its ideological premises of the pre-ordained possession of the land now known as "Canada" and, with the help of "God," to "keep our land glorious and free," we promise to "stand on guard for thee." (Stewart, 2021, p. 69)

The feelings (e.g., of belonging, loyalty) and ideas (e.g., about the legitimacy of the nation-state) produced in and through the performance of national anthems at sporting events are central to how settlers come to understand themselves in the context of the still settling state (Laurendeau, 2023, Ch. 6).

As for encounters with Indigenous mascots, I will add to the discussion above simply to note that they, too, exemplify these pedagogies of settler subjectivity, particularly in the context of youth sporting experiences (including spectatorship). King, for instance, argues that Indigenous team names and mascots teach deeply damaging lessons about race, history, and nation. Such lessons work together with those encountered in other cultural locations (you might think of tropes of Indigeneity in film and media), teaching "through complex intertextual, symbolic, and performative dialogues with other formulations of Indianness, such as movies, commodities and advertising, the news media, boy scouts and similar youth groups, biased historical accounts, and fiction" (2008, p. 150). As such, they work to "miseducate the public about cultural difference, history, race relations, and what it means to be a citizen-subject" (p. 150, emphasis his).

To reiterate, it is not simply that the tropes of Indigeneity that such mascots are "inaccurate" portrayals of Indigenous peoples and histories. Rather, they are engaged in pedagogies of how subjects (me, in this instance) understand both themselves and Others:

> ...Native American mascots always have opened as occasions for the fashioning of the self as well as the Other: they construct White citizen-subjects as proud heirs of once great people sadly gone, ...powerful conquerors and rightful owners of place and history, and men (and to a lesser extent women) privileged to honor and imitate imagined and invented alters... (King, 2008, p. 150)

These brief examples offer only glimpses of the many cultural spaces in which settlers encounter these pedagogies. In the context of *my* life, I encountered them in innumerable other sporting spaces, not to mention those encountered elsewhere in my popular cultural diet. Whether in the context of attending the Calgary Stampede, rock climbing, and studying Kinesiology at the University of

Calgary, for example, these moments were so routine and pervasive in my life that I simply failed to recognize or understand how they were teaching me (Laurendeau, 2023, Ch. 5). Looking back at them now, I see them, in Slater's terms, the "dimly lit memories" that provide clues to my developing settler subjectivity (2019, p. xii).

As I bring this chapter to a close, I invite you, reader, to consider your own encounters with pedagogies such as these. Whatever your own particular entanglements with settler colonialism, you were undoubtedly educated, perhaps unknowingly, in how to understand your place in the social world in and through your encounters with sporting spaces and institutions. Again, the various webs of settler colonialism both enable and constrain movement - of peoples *and* of ideas. They entrap some bodies and ideas, (severely) restricting their movements. Other bodies and ideas, however, are supported by various webs, allowing, even enabling, their circulation in both geographic and cultural spaces.

What kinds of lessons did you encounter in sporting spaces in your younger years? What kinds of lessons about bodies, spaces, belonging, and the nation, for instance, are among your "dimly lit memories"? In what sporting spaces did you encounter these pedagogies, and how did they shape how you came to understand yourself and your place in the world? How do they continue to do so? Finally, what might happen – how might you unsettle those pedagogies – if you were to dust off these memories and consider them in a new light?

Conclusion

As you will recall, reader, I began this chapter by asking what you think of when you hear the word genocide. My fervent hope is that you are now more attuned to the subtle ways in which genocide has unfolded and is unfolding in still-settling states, and how sport and recreation are entangled with these genocidal projects. Importantly, however, these genocidal projects are not in any way finished or uncontested. It is to this contestation, to Indigenous resistance, refusal and reterritorialization that we turn our attention in Chapter 4.

Discussion Questions

- Why do the authors of the TRC's final report suggest that residential schooling constituted *cultural genocide*? Does the distinction between genocide and cultural genocide matter? Why or why not?
- How does the sport of hockey produce a sense of belonging for (some) Canadians? Why does this sense of belonging matter in terms of settler colonialism?
- How and why did settler colonists like William George Beers colonize the game that came to be known as lacrosse?
- How are histories of land dispossession important in terms of understanding outdoor recreation in settler states like Canada?
- Why is the "control of movement [of Indigenous peoples] central to the process of colonization" (Norman et. al., 2019, p. 113)?
- How do sporting institutions and rituals contribute to settlers' sense that they are entitled do live on occupied lands? What are some of the pedagogies of settler subjectivity that produce this sense?

CHAPTER 4

Resistance, Resurgence, Reterritorialization

Introduction

What comes to mind, reader, when you think of Indigenous resistance? Perhaps you have to think for a little while before coming up with an example. Or, perhaps you reach into the cultural archive and come up with a famous example, such as the so-called "Oka crisis" (discussed below) that gripped Canada's attention in the summer of 1990. In either case, the aim in this chapter is to develop a more complex, nuanced, and multi-faceted understanding of Indigenous resistance and refusal, as well as processes of resurgence and reterritorialization. Recall the point from Chapter 1 that "[t]hose caught in the web do not simply succumb to their fate; they do their best to find or create weaknesses in the web as they fight for survival." The purpose of this chapter is to develop this idea in greater depth, highlighting how Indigenous peoples and co-conspirators both tear at the attachment points of various webs and work to build worlds not circumscribed by webs at all.

In this chapter, I take a somewhat different approach than in Chapter 3 in that I do not specifically address examples of settlers' participation in sporting organizations/initiatives. I avoid doing so in order to center the work of Indigenous peoples and organizations in the processes considered in this chapter. Another rationale for this choice is that I do not wish to offer examples that might suggest that allyship can or should take a particular shape, as this might limit the imagination of non-Indigenous peoples working to support Indigenous sovereignty. Instead, I offer some general principles outlined by McGuire-Adams in her discussion of non-Indigenous allyship. She suggests that non-Indigenous settler allies might:

- "choose to act in spaces where racism and microagression present themselves"
- "willingly enter into uncomfortable conversations with other white people [to] critically engag[e] in and [disrupt] hegemonic forms of knowledge and behaviour"
- "welcome Indigenous [peoples] to tell them when they act with microagression"
- process their own white fragility with other settler allies rather than asking this labour of Indigenous peoples
- "actively work to see where, when and how they may unknowingly reproduce whiteness and white supremacy" (2021, p. 768).

The work of settler co-conspirators towards the processes of resurgence, that is, involves important unlearning, deep introspection regarding ongoing complicity, and playing a supporting role as they imagine "opportunities to take direction from Indigenous thinkers, scholars and knowledge keepers regarding how best to amplify Indigenous practices of well-being and health" (McGuire-Adams, 2021, p. 769).

It is vital that in any interrogation of settler colonialism, we consider not only the violences that the system has wrought in the lives of Indigenous peoples in occupied territories, but also how Indigenous peoples, Nations, and organizations have refused and resisted the contours of settler colonial rule. To return to an idea from Chapter 2, one of the "normalizing narratives" that prop up settler colonialism is that Indigenous peoples are somehow *inferior*. Some observers suggest that this is a feature of Indigeneity itself – that Indigenous peoples are, by nature, "deficient" in certain respects, and as such, it is appropriate that the settler state governs most aspects of Indigenous life. The anti-Indigenous racism underlying such a position is self-evident.

Even among those much more sympathetic to the plight of Indigenous peoples, however, there is a tendency to focus only on the harms of settler colonialism, only on the damage that can be found in Indigenous lives, communities, and kinship networks. This approach is rooted, as Tuck (2009) explains, in a theory of social change suggesting that if only we can document this damage, surely political leaders will work to remedy the situation. There are two fundamental problems with this conceptualization of social change. First, there is, at this point, no reason to believe that the settler state will stop perpetuating colonial violence if only its agents better understand the plight of Indigenous peoples. The logics (e.g., the logic of elimination) underlying settler colonialism are so unshakeable as to render this a false hope. The best we might hope for if and when political leaders understand the harms experienced by Indigenous peoples is a slightly gentler system of colonial violence, still underpinned by a genocidal logic working towards the elimination of Indigenous peoples *as Indigenous peoples.*

Second, this kind of narrow focus on documenting only the damage reduces Indigenous peoples *to that damage* – it reproduces the idea that this is all we need know about Indigenous peoples. Tuck (2009) argues that while we do need to continue to document the very real harms of settler colonialism, so too do we need to understand the complexities in Indigenous lives and lifeways.

In other words, we need to know about the ways in which Indigenous peoples have and do suffer(ed) under colonial rule, but also the many examples that illustrate the refusals of Indigenous peoples to simply succumb to colonial violence. Refusals to submit to colonial rule, refusals to give up practices, ways of being and knowing, refusals to recognize the legitimacy of the settler state, even refusals to die in the face of the ongoing onslaught of settler colonialism... these too are vital to understand. It is with this vitality in mind that this chapter specifically focuses on resurgence, resistance, and reterritorialization. In the coming pages, we will consider a number of illustrative examples that point to strength, hope, and complexity in the lives of Indigenous peoples in the still-settling state.

Lacrosse

Let us return to the example of lacrosse. As noted in Chapters 2 and 3, lacrosse constitutes a key example of how settler colonizers laid claim to Indigenous sport and physical culture, reshaped it to align with their own conceptualizations of what physical cultural practices should be and do, and then deployed the newly colonized activity as part of their nation-making processes. The story does not end there, however. Indigenous peoples are not simply the victims of colonial hubris in this tale; they are important social actors themselves, working to retain and rebuild these practices on their homelands with and for each other. Moreover, as we see in the case of lacrosse, Indigenous peoples do more than work to reclaim the importance of these activities in their lives and communities; they also use them to substantiate their claims of sovereignty and nationhood.

The Haudenosaunee Nationals lacrosse team is but one example of the kinds of processes described above. Despite histories of the colonization of the game (see Chapter 3), of being prohibited from participating in an activity that had deep spiritual meaning in their Nations, Haudenosaunee peoples worked hard to reassert both their place in the game and their nationhood and sovereignty. Downey elaborates:

> For the Hodinöhsö:ni', the sport became a site of cultural resurgence within a growing pan-Indigenous movement of activism. Ousted for more than half a century, the Hodinöhsö:ni' attempted to re-enter international competition as a sovereign nation between 1983 and 1990. The Iroquois Nationals lacrosse team [since renamed the Haudenasaunee Nationals] – which represents the six nations of the Hodinöhsö:ni' Confederacy in international competition – was a conscious political effort by its organizers to assert Hodinöhsö:ni' sovereignty on the world stage and to reclaim the game of lacrosse. (2018, p. 209)

Downey stresses that the work of Haudenasaunee and other Indigenous peoples reasserting their place in the world of lacrosse must be understood relative to the broader context of Indigenous activism across Turtle Island:

> Following the introduction of controversial Indian policies in Canada, such as Pierre Elliott Trudeau's ill-fated White Paper of 1969, and the occupations of Alcatraz Island in 1969 and Wounded Knee in 1973, Indigenous communities throughout both countries united in an attempt to resist federal policies. During the 1970s, a number of Supreme Court of Canada rulings... and a rise in Indigenous activism significantly changed the state's relations with Indigenous peoples. Similarly, the United States saw a major

> increase in political mobilization by Indigenous peoples. Via the occupation of Alcatraz Island and the siege of Wounded Knee, a new group of young, active, and vocal Indigenous leaders forcefully brought attention to the conditions that Indigenous peoples across North America endured at the hands of the dominant societies and their colonial governments. (2018, pp. 209-210)

Similar sensibilities that underpinned these vital acts of resistance and resurgence can be seen in the trajectory of the Haudenosaunee Nationals, and some of the leaders of these acts of refusal were instrumental in the revival of lacrosse in Haudenosaunee territories.

The Haudenasaunee sent a delegation to Wounded Knee, one led by Oren Lyons, Faithkeeper and former National Collegiate Athletic Association college lacrosse player. Lyons would go on to play an important role in resolving a high-profile dispute over sacred lands in Kanehsatà:ke territory and in the formation of the Haudenasaunee Nationals, both of which should be understood in terms of the broader movement of Indigenous peoples described above (Downey, 2018).

In 1990, Kanien'kehaka (Mohawk) peoples, along with their allies across Turtle Island, engaged in direct action to protest the extension of a golf course into sacred burial grounds (what the mainstream press would too easily call "contested" lands). In short, the people of Kanehsatà:ke stood up "against the government and their security forces with nothing but their spirituality and hope [and defeated] the Federal government of Canada" (O'Bonsawin, 2017, p. 420). As Ladner and Simpson (2010) elaborate:

> The summer of 1990 brought some strong medicine to Turtle Island. For many Canadians, "Oka" was the first time they encountered

Resistance, Resurgence, Reterritorialization

> Indigenous anger, resistance and standoff, and the resistance was quickly dubbed both the "Oka Crisis" and the "Oka Crises" by the mainstream media. But to the Kanien'kehaka (Mohawk) people of Kanehsata:ke, who were living up to their responsibilities to take care of their lands, this was neither a "crisis" at Oka, nor was it about the non-Native town of "Oka." This was about 400 years of colonial injustice... This was about 400 years of resistance... It was not a beginning. Nor was this the end. This was the culmination of many, many years of Onhkwehonwe resistance resulting in a decision to put up barricades in defense of, and to bring attention to, Haudenosaunee land ethics, treaty responsibilities and governance. (p. 1)

In this excerpt, Ladner and Simpson emphasize the value in interrogating mainstream media accounts (and, for that matter, history

"oka-crisis" by Injuneering is marked with Public Domain Mark 1.0.

textbooks) and how they frame important events such as this vital act of refusal. They continue:

> Although the mainstream media focused on the white town of "Oka" and the "warriors," the Kanien'kehaka resistance was envisioned and carried out by Kanien'kehaka people from Kanehsatka:ke, Kahnawa:ke and Akwesasne... True, it was a critical act of resistance, but it was also a vision of reclamation, revitalization and restoration of Haudenosaunee lands, treaties, political traditions and responsibilities. (pp. 1-2)

Ladner and Simpson draw our attention to the notion that this vital act of resistance was not simply *against* something (e.g., the settler state and racial capitalism), but was an act of upholding the "traditions and responsibilities" of these communities *"as [they] have always done"* (L. Simpson, 2017). Not only, then, does the Kanehsatà:ke resistance illustrate refusal (to acquiesce to colonial rule), but analyses such as that offered by Ladner and Simpson similarly refuse colonial framings of these pivotal events.

There are several connections between sport and settler colonialism in this particular story, two of which are worth mentioning here. First, sport is near the centre of these events since it was the expansion of a golf course that sparked the standoff. Second, Oren Lyons was "a key negotiator... helping to bring the invasion of Kanehsatà:ke to an end" (Downey, 2018, pp. 248-249). This was amidst his intense involvement in asserting nationhood and sovereignty as a vital force with the Haudenasaunee Nationals. Lyons, along with Skarù·rę? Nation (Tuscarora) members Rick Hill, Wes Patterson, and Carol Patterson, took a deeply political approach with this team as they worked towards their acceptance in the international lacrosse community. They argued that "the Nationals were to be accepted in international competition as representatives of the distinct and sovereign Hodinöhsö:ni' Nation – or not at all" (Downey, 2018, p. 213).

One important strategy by which the Nationals pursued this agenda was through passports. Members travelled not using Canadian or US passports, but on the *Haudenosaunee* passport. This passport has a history dating back to the early 1920s and has always constituted an assertion of the Nation's self-determination, so its use by the Nationals is unquestionably both purposeful and political (Downey, 2018). Lyons and the other organizers believed in the power of lacrosse as a healing game, understood the rough political waters into which they were wading, and positioned both the team and the game to contribute to their political goals (Downey, 2018). As Downey puts it, the team "was an example of what Audra Simpson masterfully demonstrates in Mohawk Interruptus as an articulation of Hodinöhsö:ni' self-determination 'in ways that refuse the absolute sovereignty of at least two settler states'" (2018, p. 211). This "refusal of the absolute sovereignty" of Canada and the U.S. constitutes an important example of Indigenous efforts to weaken and fray the threads of settler colonialism that reach into their lives and communities.

The Nationals worked not only towards *external* assertions of sovereignty and nationhood, but also to strengthening internal relations between Nations. As Downey explains,

> [w]hereas the establishment of the Iroquois Nationals was a political strategy for the assertion of Hodinöhsö:ni' sovereignty, it was equally an instrument for traditionalists to strengthen cultural unification and the Longhouse resurgence between Hodinöhsö:ni' communities. Quite simply, the team became a contemporary act of Hodinöhsö:ni' socio-political and cultural revival; it was an example of the use of traditionalism as an organizing tool for the articulation of self-determination. (2018, p. 216)

In other words, the formation of the Haudenosaunee Nationals simultaneously worked externally to strengthen claims to nationhood and sovereignty and internally to bolster efforts to renew ties and political cooperation between clans in the Confederacy.

The emergence of the team was not without political challenges and tensions. There were many practical barriers and questions that had to be negotiated along the way, including: 1) Whether women could form a team, a debate that included disagreements between different clans (and between modernists and traditionalists); 2) Whether only Haudenosaunee men could play on the men's team, or whether it would be opened up more broadly (to Squamish men, for instance – Downey, 2018). These tensions, however, do not undermine the political importance of both lacrosse and the Nationals to processes of resurgence. Rather, they highlight the complexities in and between Indigenous Nations and worldviews. They paint, in other words, more complex pictures of Indigenous lives, histories, and politics – it is this complexity that works to refuse the kinds of "damage-centred" stories against which Tuck (2009) cautions. In other words, complex narratives such as this one work to refuse the kinds of "normalizing narratives" we encounter in so many cultural spaces.

Reterritorialization

As highlighted throughout this book, land is at the very centre of the settler colonial project. Moreover, a key part of the project of reasserting claims to land in perpetuity is attacking the connections between Indigenous peoples and the lands for which they have cared since time immemorial. This takes many forms, as discussed above. To set the stage for a discussion of reterritorialization, however, it is worth revisiting this point. Here I draw on the words of settler scholar Sam McKegney to reiterate the vital connections between bodies and lands in all of this: "...the fracturing of mind and body... is a key weapon within the dispossessive arsenal of Canadian colonial policy, which seeks to deterritorialize Indigenous nations and corrode Indigenous sovereignties by compromising embodied connections to place and to kin" (2013, p. 23). I hope, reader, that you hear the parallels between McKegney's words and the discussion of the logic of containment in Chapter 3. The point, in both instances, is that colonial policy and practice specifically targets these "embodied connections" as part of its genocidal project; to the extent that it can rupture these connections between Indigenous bodies and Indigenous lands, the settler state can continue to claim those same lands towards the project of capital accumulation in the new social order.

In the face of attacks such as those outlined above, *reterritorialization* refers to the processes by which Indigenous peoples and Nations reassert connections to their homelands, connections specifically and repeatedly targeted by the settler state. McKegney explains it as a process that "honours and reclaims the land through embodied discursive actions that simultaneously honour and reclaim the body" (2013, p. 28). Such processes can unfold at multiple levels as Nations, individuals, and kinship networks work to strengthen and rebuild these connections so vital to their lives, spiritualities, and livelihoods. In the realm of sport and physical activity, such processes include any practices – individual or collective, organized or otherwise – that deepen embodied connections to lands and waters.

McKegney draws on the example of the Residential School Walkers, a collection of young Indigenous men (most of them Cree) who walked approximately 2,200 km from Northern Ontario to a TRC event in Halifax, Nova Scotia, in support of those testifying at these events and residential school survivors more generally. This walk, McKegney argues, exemplifies processes that "reaffirm bonds of kinship and enact cross-gender solidarities that might encourage Indigenous reterritorialization" (2013, p. 14). More specifically, he suggests that these young men "honoured the body as integral to and indivisible from the agentic self," affirmed "responsibilities to and roles within the family" (with family defined in terms of Cree knowledge systems), and reconnected "with the land as an active principle of kinship" (26). This walk – and other processes of reterritorialization – thus serve(d) to strengthen connections between Indigenous peoples and their bodies, their kin, and the lands themselves, thus constituting an explicit refusal of colonial logics of containment. For Indigenous peoples – who have so regularly had imposed upon them forms of movement, (non-)relations with each other, and disconnection from their lands – to actively choose such an extraordinary act of love for themselves, their people, and their homelands, is a radical act indeed.

McGuire-Adams and Giles's research with Anishinaabekweg (Anishinaabe women) and their dibaajimowinan (stories) of long-distance running is instructive in this consideration of reterritorialization. These women, McGuire-Adams and Giles argue, "showcase a strengths-based resistance to the impacts of colonialism and are decolonizing by mindfully connecting to their physical activity to ceremony, healing, inspiring others, and achieving personal health and wellbeing" (2018, p. 212). The connections to territory are particularly important in these Anishinaabekweg's dibaajimowinan as they emphasize that running on their own homelands with their lands and cultures clearly in mind constitutes "a process of healing, regeneration, and a reconnection to lands, and therefore, [challenges] settler colonialism" (2018, p. 212). Note, in McGuire-Adams and Giles' research, the centrality of re-establishing and strengthening connections to and relations with the lands, community, and culture:

> Anishinaabeg health and wellbeing is fundamentally connected to our territories; territories contain ancestral stories and are imbued with Anishinaabeg reciprocal relationships to all animate beings; territories are where Anishinaabeg identities, culture, teachings, and stories are found. This is why the research participants spoke about how they find healing while running and by reconnecting to their territories and, in so doing, the women create a community committed to health and wellbeing; the act of running on the land, thus, represences Anishinaabeg on the land, which also fosters personal decolonization through physical activity, and creates a community of support. (2018, p. 212)

It is worth lingering, here, with the idea of *represencing*. The active verb pointing to the conscious and purposeful reassertion of Indigenous (Anishinaabe, in this instance) presence on lands claimed by Canada stands in direct opposition to the foundational aims of settler colonialism. It fostered in the runners themselves connections to territory and kin (through the offering of prayers, for example), as well as increasing the visibility of Indigenous peoples on the very lands from which they have been displaced by so many colonial policies and practices.

Reserves/Reservations and Sovereignty

As noted in Chapter 3, reserves (the language in the Canadian context) are spaces central to the logics of containment and elimination described throughout this book. As settler states assumed ownership of enormous swathes of land across Turtle Island, they often relegated First Nations peoples to small parcels of land, thereby largely removing them from other lands that could then be "developed" in accordance with colonial logics. It is vital to note that many Indigenous peoples do not live on reserves; in Canada, for example, census data indicate that urban Indigenous peoples comprise approximately 45% of all Indigenous peoples [see digital repository, "Indigenous Population Continues to Grow"], and Metis and Inuit do not have reserve lands. Nevertheless, these spaces denoted by the settler state *as Indigenous spaces* are central to the settler colonial project, created and administrated by the settler state in keeping with the ongoing project of settler colonialism.

At the same time, however, reserves have always been spaces in which Indigenous resurgence, revitalization, and refusal can be fostered. Furthermore, despite colonial efforts of containment and assimilation, sport has and continues to play a vital role in such spaces: "…Indigenous sport is integral in instilling Indigenous values, knowledge, and community connectedness necessary for Indigenous nations to survive endemic hardships" (Leonard et al., 2021, p. 236). Paradoxically, then, "the reserve" is both a key web weaponized in settler state policy and practice *and* a space in which Indigenous peoples (re)build community, refuse settler colonial logics, and protect themselves against the many violences woven into their lives and social worlds (Norman et al., 2022).

Among the violences referred to above is the COVID-19 pandemic, which disproportionately impacted Indigenous peoples. In a recent chapter about the impacts of the pandemic in Indigenous communities, Kelsey Leonard (Shinnecock Nation), Natalie Welch (Eastern Band of Cherokee Indians) and Alisse Ali-Joseph (Choctaw Nation of Oklahoma) take an "abundance-based" approach, focusing on "protective factors… including community, relationality, abundance, strength, and resilience that protect

Indigenous athletes and communities from stressors like the pandemic" (2021, pp. 236-237). They interrogate the part these interconnected protective factors play in the exercising of sovereignty on Indigenous lands. In the broader picture, they argue, exercising sovereignty in these ways is part of Indigenous *survivance*, or "the continuity of Indigenous peoples and societies through conscious and self-determined practices of resistance and survival" (p. 237).

The protective factor of community, Leonard and colleagues note, is evident in shared passions for sport such as "Rez ball... a unique form of basketball developed on reserves and reservations across Indian country" (2021, p. 238). "Rez ball" is an "up-tempo style of [basketball] that developed in Indian [residential] schools and later evolved" as it was played in Indigenous communities (Davies, 2020, p. 5.) Community is vital in the sense that individual communities can put into place protective measures such as refusing entry to non-residents. They note that in the early days of the COVID-19 pandemic, this allowed some First Nations to create safe(r) spaces in their communities for people to get outside and reconnect with the land during those uncertain days "without the risk of heavy tourist traffic normally brings" (p. 239). Relationality and strength, Leonard and colleagues note, are evident in numerous ways, not least through the initiatives taken to move important social gatherings and fitness classes to online platforms as the effects of the pandemic became evident. They point to a Facebook group called "Social Distance Powwow" as an example, "celebrating the beauty of Indigenous dance and song, while ultimately building an unprecedented sense of Indigenous belonging through new media" (240). Online fitness classes, too, allowed for continued connections to kin and community to be fostered at the same time as they centered physical activity when staying active was deeply challenging amidst the uncertainty.

Abundance, Leonard et. al. note, is central to Indigenous communities. This was evident in the early days of the pandemic, for example, when high-profile Indigenous athletes and organizations worked hard to ensure that food, money, and other necessities were delivered to those Indigenous communities hardest hit by the first wave of COVID-19 infections and those most in need of support more generally. Finally, these researchers highlight the resilience evident in the messaging about health (broadly conceived) that proliferated early in the pandemic. These included campaigns encouraging athletes to stay active *while protecting the health of elders* and emphasizing the healing inextricably embedded in activities such as the Jingle Dress dance (Anishinaabe) or Fire Ball (e.g., Mashpee Wampanoag), "a ceremonial game where a ball traditionally made out of deerskin is soaked in whale oil and lit on fire as players toss and kick the ball across the playing field" (Leonard et al., 2021, p. 243). Such initiatives emphasize the point made about lacrosse – in the context of Indigenous communities, sport is more than *just* sport; it is also always about community, healing, and strength (Leonard et al., 2021).

To further flesh out the idea of reserves as spaces for the production of sovereignty, let us return to the discussion of minor hockey from Chapter 3. Recall some of the tensions at play, and the colonial logics at work, in the disbanding of Indigenous teams and the racial divide in Manitoba. Here, our focus is on the strength and resurgence made evident by teams based in Indigenous communities. As Norman and colleagues highlight, "reserves are places that are intimately interwoven with family, community, culture, in many cases traditional and ancestral lands, and ultimately nationhood" (2022, p. 328). As noted in Chapter 3, then, teams connected to reserves are important vehicles for reaffirming connections to kin, to territory, and to nationhood. Not only do they give Indigenous athletes the opportunity to "bring their full selves into the dressing room" (McKegney et. al., 2021, p. 32), but they contribute to the very protective factors outlined by Leonard, Welch, and Ali-Joseph; they exemplify the exercising of sovereignty these authors describe. Indeed, Norman and colleagues refer to this as "embodied Indigenous sovereignty," noting that Indigenous players playing on their own homelands *embody* the land and thus challenge settler authority and settler colonial logics themselves.

"Bluespaces"

Connections to territory, space, and culture include not only lands but also waters, or what Olive and Wheaton describe as "blue spaces" that include "waterscapes and their surroundings" (2021, p. 4). Writing from Aotearoa/New Zealand, for example, Waiti and Wheaton take up the question of Māori practices of resurgence, emphasizing that "[w]aterways including rivers, lakes and the ocean are regarded by Māori as a taonga (treasure), reflecting the concept of whakapapa (genealogy) and connection to place" (2022, p. 85). These researchers consider how present-day Māori "continue to enact and revive their associations with the ocean through the revival of traditional concepts, customs and knowledge," many of which have been under attack since the arrival of European settlers in the late 1700s. They document how these processes of revitalization of culture and connection to place and ancestry unfold in the context of three ocean-based recreational activities that, together, encompass the various "domains" of the ocean: the shorelines, coastal waters, and open ocean.

Waka hourua are double-hulled voyaging canoes that link Māori to what are arguably "the most dramatic burst of overwater exploration in human prehistory," (Waiti & Wheaton, 2022, p. 90) including the sophisticated navigational knowledge that allowed Māori to populate Aotearoa between 800-1350 AD. In recent years, there has been a notable resurgence in this open-ocean activity, as Waiti and Wheaton explain:

> Many iwi [tribe] and Māori organizations throughout Aotearoa NZ have now acquired or built their own waka hourua to help promote Mātauranga whakatere waka [Māori navigation knowledge systems] and cultural development… Some [voyaging societies] are using their waka hourua as 'floating classrooms', whereby the waka and associated Mātauranga whakatere waka… are used to disseminate cultural knowledges and practices. (91)

Waka ama (outrigger canoeing) has seen a tremendous expansion in recent years, and has particularly drawn Māori women into an increasingly organized and commercialized competitive coastal-water sport. As Waiti and Wheaton emphasize, however, for Māori, "'sport' often takes different meaning than maximising the performance [with] spiritual development considered as important as the physical pursuit" (2022, p. 92). These researchers and others highlight how Māori have engaged with waka ama not only as a recreational and/or competitive activity, but also as a way of experiencing "embodied, emotional, and spiritual connections with their ancestry, colonial history, nature, and other people" (2022, p. 92). Drawing on ethnographic research, Liu interrogates how participation in waka ama becomes a site for the reproduction of Māori knowledge, culture, and history, including through ritual chants or prayers known as karakia, that "recognizes the ocean bluespace as an active player in human-nature interaction," an "entanglement [that is] both spiritual and physical" (2021, pp. 146-147). Liu's research participants also describe their "sensuous" encounters with the bluespace as the "ocean becomes more than a geographical feature of the earth or a huge body of water, but a relationally, historically, culturally, spiritually, and sensuously meaningful bluespace for Māori participants" (Liu, 2021, p. 149). Taken together, these studies support Wikaire and Newman's suggestion that waka ama is "a site of resistance to, and potentially productive formation within, contemporary neocolonial Aotearoa/New Zealand" (2013, p. 60). This is not to suggest, however, that waka ama is an *uncomplicated* site of resistance. Particularly as corporate and market forces and logics shape a burgeoning sport such as waka ama, this is sure to shape "the sport's framing of, and productive capacities for, *tino-rangatiratanga* [Māori self-determination]" (Wikaire & Newman, 2013, p. 61).

Heke ngaru (surfing) is the third water-based activity that Waiti and Wheaton describe as making a resurgence among Māori in Aotearoa. They argue that though surfing has long histories among Māori peoples, having been practiced by all ages and genders, the pressures of colonisation dramatically decreased Māori heke ngaru until recent decades. They describe the recent prominence and success of many Māori surfers in both national and international competition, and note that national competitions, in particular, have allowed "Māori wave riders to reaffirm and connect with whakapapa whānau [genealogy] and kaupapa whanau (i.e., other Māori surfers). It demonstrates also the connection between knowledge and practice in contemporary surfing activities" (pp. 93-94). Waiti and Awatere elaborate on these connections in their discussion of "Māori surfers' (kaihekengaru) perceptions of a sense of place" (2019, p. 35):

> kaihekengaru experience a sense of place which is underpinned by mātauranga Māori [traditional knowledge systems] and a Māori

worldview. The sense of place for these kaihekengaru reflects both the ocean and nearby landmarks. Drawing on the concept of whakapapa [genealogy], surfing enables these kaihekengaru to connect with iwi-specific environmental features, their ancestors and the various Ātua [gods, deitys]. Surfing re-affirms their whakapapa as they are imbued in the environment, immersed in the ocean, and acknowledging the deeds of their ancestors. In this sense, "being Māori is felt, embodied, and emplaced"… (2019, p. 40)

Indigenous-Organized Sports/Games/Festivals

I noted in Chapters 2 and 3 that in the settler state, organization of and funding for Indigenous sport generally adhere to a colonial logic and thus constitute key elements of to the network of webs of settler colonialism. Yet in Chapter 4, I have enumerated a number of cases that illustrate the value of Indigenous leadership and organization, not only for Indigenous athletes but for broader processes of renewal and resurgence. Here, I develop this point further in two directions.

First, let us consider the example of a high-level organization working to both provide leadership for Indigenous sport and to remind those in the mainstream sport system of the importance of such leadership. The Aboriginal Sport Circle (ASC) arose in the 1990s during a moment of considerable attention being devoted to the relationship between Canada and Indigenous peoples (recall that the Kanehsatà:ke Resistance took place in 1990, which incited much – though arguably not enough – reflection). Alwyn Morris (a member of the Kahnawake Nation) was a decorated Olympian and a force in the development of an Indigenous sport system. He directed "talks with political leaders, coordinated discussions among mainstream sport organizations, and took every opportunity he could to make sure Indigenous sport was a government priority" (Forsyth, 2020, p. 119). Taken together, the events at Kanehsatà:ke, numerous government processes examining sport leadership and organization, and the initiative of powerful Indigenous leaders (not only Morris, but others like Wilton Littlechild), laid the foundation for the ASC to be established in 1995 (Forsyth, 2020).

The ASC draws on the metaphor of a double helix to conceptualize the relationship between the mainstream sport system and the Indigenous sport system. The double helix, ASC members have asserted, is a useful metaphor as it is one with which mainstream sport leaders are familiar. As such, it translates in a fairly straightforward way *while emphasizing the point that the two systems are and should be somewhat distinct* (Forsyth, 2020). This model was meant to illustrate the importance Indigenous sport leaders had long been attaching to Indigenous leadership:

> For nearly twenty-five years, Indigenous sport leaders had been trying to build the Indigenous sport system in Canada and provide opportunities for Indigenous athletes to integrate into mainstream sport if they so desired. Equally important, they had been working towards these goals in ways that contributed to Indigenous self-determination by fostering a greater appreciation of their cultures and identities, and, in some cases, their continued connections to the land. (Forsyth, 2020, p. 124)

As noted in Chapter 1, games and festivals organized by and for Indigenous peoples constitute another example of Indigenous resurgence. Depending on the particular context, such events work to strengthen a number of dimensions of Indigenous revitalization, including fostering organizational capacity, creating and deepening connections between Indigenous peoples at multiple levels, and re-establishing or strengthening connections to kin, lands, and culture. The NAIG exemplifies all of these dimensions, constituting "a major sporting and cultural festival for Indigenous people in Canada and the United States, [and] the most visible expression of the double helix model" (Forsyth, 2020, p. 125).

As important as the NAIG has been and continues to be, it is vital to recognize that there are numerous other Indigenous-led and organized festivals, including the World Indigenous Nations Games (e.g., Chen, Mason, & Misener, 2022), the Dene Games (e.g., Giles, 2008), and many others more localized in nature. For an example of the latter, consider Skogvang's investigation of a Sámi festival in Norway called Riddu Riđđu:

> The young Sámi people who started Riddu Riđđu have done a great deal to restore pride in their ancestral culture. The festival also been used by the organizers, to teach children about their ancestral culture, and to be proud of it. The people organizing the festival have been able to create an opportunity for exchange between [I]ndigenous peoples. (2021, p. 367)

Festivals and organized events such as these work to refuse the logics of settler colonialism by (re)establishing and strengthening the very elements of Indigenous life (e.g., self-determination, connection to kin and territory, language, culture) targeted in and by the settler state and its many webs.

"Personal Decolonization"

McGuire-Adams (2020) makes a compelling and urgent argument that settler colonialism is *embodied*. It lives in the bodies of those targeted by the settler state, evident, for instance, in relatively low levels of health among Indigenous peoples in general. This ill health, McGuire-Adams emphasizes, is not a manifestation of poor individual choices (as neoliberal framings would suggest) but rather an outcome of the violences of settler colonialism – the webs *produce* these poor health outcomes. In light of the regularity and depth of the traumas of settler colonialism, it is no wonder, McGuire-Adams highlights, that Indigenous peoples have relatively poor health outcomes. What's more, she argues that this is particularly true – and particularly troubling – for Indigenous women. Indigenous women, she suggests, embody a particular threat to settler colonialism, and as such are especially important targets of colonial violence: "Indigenous women are intrinsically connected to the land… [so] we are seen as credible threats to ongoing settler entitlement to Indigenous Territories and are actively targeted for silence, even death" (2020, p. 32). Under such conditions, one important dimension of resurgence is the efforts Indigenous women, in particular, are making towards what McGuire-Adams calls "personal decolonization." She notes that colonialism lives not only in Indigenous bodies but also Indigenous minds; as such, physical activity that dislodges colonial narratives constitutes a vital act of refusal: refusal to believe the stories told about oneself and one's people. McGuire-Adams' research participants – whether engaged in running or kettle-bell workouts, for example – were thus fostering personal decolonization that not only benefits their own health but also reverberates more broadly:

> The women all spoke about the need to be healthy for themselves, for their children, and to provide examples of living well for their communities. This shows that they are aware of the settler-colonial deficit analysis that pathologizes them as ill, as if illness is inevitable, but they are challenging it by choosing to be healthy for themselves, which then reverberates to their families and communities. (2020, p. 79)

Such personal decolonization, in other words, is much more than personal. Through their physical activity, these women refuse the pathologizing narrative about Indigenous women, set examples for their loved ones and communities, and (re)build strength at all of these levels.

Conclusion

In this chapter, I presented a number of examples illustrating strength, capacity, complexity, and desire in Indigenous lives, kinship networks, and Nations. I have touched on but a few of the many examples that point to Indigenous refusal and resurgence in and through sport and physical activity. There are many more examples to be found, including organized opposition to mega-events (e.g., O'Bonsawin, 2010), legal proceedings towards reclaiming stewardship over mountain spaces (e.g., Mason et. al., 2022), and many others. Each of these examples challenges the "normalizing narratives" of settler colonialism, and thus challenges settler colonialism itself. In the next and final chapter, I draw together some of the most important threads running through this work, return to key questions I posed in Chapter 1, and offer some reflections on the importance of continuing to learn about sport, recreation, and settler colonialism.

Discussion Questions

- How does the story of the Haudenosaunee Nationals illustrate Indigenous refusal and resurgence?
- What is "reterritorialization" and how does it challenge ongoing processes of colonial violence?

- In what sense are reserves spaces for fostering Indigenous sovereignty?
- What are "bluespaces" and how are they related to Indigenous resurgence?
- How does the ASC's use of the double-helix metaphor challenge settler colonial governance of sport in Canada?
- What is "personal decolonization" and how does it contribute to broader processes of resurgence?

CHAPTER 5

Summary and Conclusions

Returning to Where we Started

The point of studying something, in my view, is to come to appreciate how little we know, perhaps even how little we *can* know. The point of the exercise is not to tick off a number of learning boxes along the way until we have "finished learning." If something is worth learning, it is worth thinking about deeply in order to appreciate the limits of our understanding, to expand those limits to the extent that this is possible, and to respect that we simply cannot know everything. My hope is that by this point you share my view that the topic of sport and settler colonialism is very much worth learning in this way. The object is not to understand with perfect clarity exactly what sport means in the lives of Indigenous peoples, nor in the lives of settlers. Rather, the object is to be in a better position to understand the layers, the contradictions – the webs – how all of this is connected to both the material realities of people and the ideas that circulate in particular cultural spaces. In that sense, there is *always* more to learn. Each time I teach a course on sport and settler colonialism, each time I have a conversation about these topics with friends, colleagues, and research collaborators, I seek to appreciate new layers, to ask new questions, to better understand the importance of such inquiries.

It is not simply a matter of learning. It is also important to unlearn some of the taken-for-granted ideas that we encounter. Certainly, it is vital to unlearn the stereotypes that circulate in culture. It is just as imperative, however, to unlearn our assumptions about policy, academic knowledge, and more. In the realm of academia, it is helpful to recall that universities themselves are part of the network of colonial insitutions in still-settling states. This will help us to question and interrogate the concepts, geographies, and cultural ideas we encounter in these spaces of "higher learning" and recall that all knowledge is situated, shaped by systems of power and privilege.

As I write these words (December 2022), I'm sitting at an outdoor café in Sapporo, Japan. Living in Hokkaido for a little over three months this fall has had me asking new questions about the shape that settler colonialism takes here in a context that both parallels Canadian settler colonialism in key ways (e.g., Hokkaido was folded into the new, modern Japan at almost exactly the same moment that Canada came to be as a nation-state by that name) and diverges from it in others, as I briefly noted in Chapter 1. I have much to learn about settler colonialism here and in other contexts. In the current moment, I am especially motivated to learn more about settler colonialism in Hokkaido, not only to better understand these histories and presents, but to think through my own responsibilities as a temporary settler on these lands. My point, simply, is that I hope that the work that you have encountered in these pages has motivated you to continue to interrogate your social world with a specific focus on settler colonialism. I hope that the end of this book, in other words, represents not the *end* of your learning but the *beginning*.

In particular, if you are a settler, the single thing that would best indicate that we have both done our jobs is if you find yourself more motivated to think "through the term 'settler' as a set of

Summary and Conclusions

responsibilities and action" (Flowers, 2015, p. 33), asking what *your* responsibilities are or might be and how to go about putting them into action. My hope more generally is that having engaged with the work in these pages you better understand the network of webs, where and how they live in your own life, what it means to live in relation to those webs, and, perhaps, how you might do so differently in light of the work we have done together.

You will recall, reader, that I posed a number of questions to you in the opening chapters of this book. At the start of this final chapter, I invite you to consider them anew in light of the work with which you have engaged in these pages.

What comes to mind *now* when you hear the term settler colonialism? Whatever your starting point when you first opened this book, I hope that you now feel more confident in naming settler colonialism. I hope you understand it as the underlying foundation of settler states, as a system of social organization (a network of webs) predicated on land dispossession and the replacement of existing social orders with new, colonial institutions and worldviews that are very much alive in the present. Moreover, I hope that you appreciate more deeply the sense in which settler colonialism is inextricably *relational*, structuring the lives of all who live in occupied territories in ways that are deeply connected to one another.

How would you articulate the connections between sport and settler colonialism? At the outset of this book, perhaps you were unsure of where and how sport and settler colonialism intersect. By now, you should be better able to point out how sport and settler colonialism are mutually constitutive in settler states. If I have done my job in these pages (and you yours), you should better understand sport and recreation as both shaped by and productive of how we think about ourselves, each other, bodies and embodiment, lands and waters, "resources," the settler-state, settler-Indigenous relations, and more. You should also better appreciate the nuances of sport and recreation as sites of both settler colonial violence and Indigenous resistance and resurgence.

Lastly, but perhaps most importantly, what are your own entanglements with settler colonialism, particularly in the realm of sport and physical culture? In what ways is your life structured by settler colonialism and how does that show up in your recreational and sporting pursuits? In what ways do you perpetuate and/or challenge colonial logics in and through your physical cultural pursuits? As I emphasized in Chapter 1, understanding the interconnections between sport and settler colonialism is not an intellectual exercise; it is part of understanding the social worlds in which we are embedded as well as those we are helping to (re)build. What kind of world do *you* want to help build? Whose lives will it shape and in what ways? These questions are foundational to studying these ideas and should, in my estimation, be the very reason for doing this work.

Re-creation

As I draw this work to a close, I want to return to the title of the book: *Settler Colonialism, Sport, and Recreation*. We've considered sport and settler colonialism in some depth in these pages and have touched on recreation throughout. What we have yet to consider is *re-creation*. In particular, I want to draw to the surface two treatments of the idea for how, together, they encapsulate much of the work we have done together. The first comes from the Royal Commission on Aboriginal Peoples (RCAP), undertaken in Canada in the wake of the Kanehsatà:ke Resistance of 1990. Writing about sport in residential schools, the report's authors note: "In school, in chapel, at work and even at play the children were to learn the Canadian way. *Recreation was re-creation*" (cited in Downey, 2018, p. 99, emphasis added). In this quote from the RCAP, we see the idea that sport was being used to *remake* Indigenous youth as part of an assimilatory project.

The second engagement with the idea of recreation comes from Leanne Betasamosake Simpson, who references the Seven Fires Prophecy, an important element of Nishnaabeg thought. The prophecy tells of an era (many believe this to be the current era) in which "people would begin to emerge who would be concerned with healing the broken relationships born of the past [and] learn how to re-engage in relationships at all scales in healthy and balanced ways" (Pyne, 2014, p. 16). Importantly, the prophecy refers not only to choices made by the Anishinaabek, but settlers' choices as well, "making the Seven Fires Prophecy a valuable interpretative framework for understanding how to reconcile relationships between the Anishinaabek and the newcomers to Turtle Island" (Pyne, 2014, p. 16). Building on this understanding, Simpson explains:

> In the last section of the Seven Fires Prophecy, there is a mirroring of the cycle of creation-destruction-re-creation within Nishnaabeg thought. The cycle sets the stage for interpretation of *re-creation as a new emergence or resurgence*... Within Nishnaabeg thought, there is not a singular vision of resurgence, but many. (2011, p. 68, emphasis added)

Whereas the RCAP quote references sport as an assimilatory tool, Simpson's quote draws attention to re-creation as a generative and necessary process of resurgence that takes many forms and works towards healing and relationality for all who share these lands. Together, it seems to me, these ideas convey the heart of the connection between sport and settler colonialism; sport is both a cultural locale in which settler colonialism works according to the logic of elimination *and* one in which Indigenous peoples and co-conspirators creatively resist and reimagine life in and beyond settler colonialism. In that sense, this book *could* be titled *Settler Colonialism, Sport, and Re-creation*. But we needed to do some work together to arrive at this understanding, so I offer it now in the hopes that you are better equipped to appreciate the nuances of this framing.

Conclusion

I have asked a great deal from you in these pages, reader. I understand that, and while I make no apology for challenging you to take on this work that is difficult both intellectually and emotionally, I want to leave you with something hopeful.

As I have emphasized repeatedly in these pages, settler colonialism is not a one-time event but an ongoing set of structures and practices always working towards its own reproduction, always working towards the ongoing dispossession of lands from those who have long been stewards of the same lands.

That is not the hopeful part.

The hopeful part is that resistance, too, is an ongoing project. Refusal, reimagination, reterritorialization. Indigenous peoples have always resisted colonial rule, both in obvious ways such as the Kanehsatà:ke Resistance and in more everyday ways such as language revitalization, the passing on of cultural knowledge, the teaching of practices such as hunting and trapping, or simply surviving in the face of coordinated attacks on lives, lands, Nations, and kinship networks. Simpson and Ladner articulate this beautifully:

> The ancestors not only fought, blockaded, protested and mobilized against these forces on every Indigenous territory on Turtle

> Island, they also engaged in countless acts of hidden resistance and kitchen table resistance aimed at ensuring their children and grandchildren could live as Indigenous peoples. (2010, p. 8, emphasis in original)

These forms of hidden and "kitchen table" resistance, too, offer reason for hope. Hope that settler states structured according to logics that both necessitate and produce inextricably uneven social relations are not the only futures that can be envisioned. Hope that very different kinds of social organization are possible. Hope that the work that many Indigenous peoples have long been doing, and that a growing number of co-conspirators are working to support, can show us a different world, a future anchored not by systemic inequality and violence but by communities of care. It is toward such futures that we see what Leanne Simpson (2017) calls "constellations of co-resistance" working.

When I teach a course on sport and settler colonialism, the question I hear most often – especially from settler student-scholars – is this: What can I do? I imagine that some readers might have the same question. It's an important one and one I ask myself on a regular basis. Here, I will refuse to answer the question directly and challenge you, instead, to ask yourself what *you* can do. If engaging with this work has convinced you that settler colonialism is a deep and abiding problem in settler states, if your own entanglements with settler colonialism now have you feeling unsettled, then I am happy. I am not happy *that* you feel unsettled, but that such a feeling can help us think through our particular social worlds, the particular shapes that our complicity takes, the particular courses of (in)action we might pursue towards dismantling these violent systems. I invite you to think through your own refusals, for instance. You might refuse to let a loved one's problematic comments go unchallenged, refuse to stand for the national anthem, or refuse to let the whiteness of another course outline go unchallenged, for instance. I also invite you to consider where you are investing your time as well as your intellectual and emotional energies. How might you do more to "live in Indigenous sovereignty," as Carlson Manathara (2021) puts it?

Again, I offer these invitations and challenges not because I have this all figured out. I offer them in solidarity, as someone routinely asking himself the same questions. The point, again, is not to follow some "best practices" guide in order to better negotiate the contours of settler colonialism. Rather, the point is to work towards a future not structured by settler colonialism at all. Perhaps, like me, you have no idea how, specifically, to do so. But isn't that a question worth asking, worth centering in our lives? Isn't it worth asking, as Cree scholar Dallas Hunt does: "If futures are not circumscribed by the parameters of settler colonialism, where, in fact, will we go?" (2018, p. 84).

Discussion Questions

- What does it mean to think "through the term 'settler' as a set of responsibilities and action" (Flowers, 2015, p. 33)?
- Why is it important to interrogate how settler colonialism structures "the lives of all who live in occupied territories"?
- In what sense(s) does the idea of "re-creation" highlight key tensions in our discussion of sport and settler colonialism?
- In a consideration of a genocidal project like settler colonialism, where are we to find hope?

NOTE

Chapter 1: Introduction

1. In settler states like Canada, Treaties are complicated "agreements" indeed; I do not mean here to reify treaties or suggest in any way that they constitute(d) a straightforward transfer of lands/waters/etc. For more on the so-called "numbered Treaties," see Krasowski, 2019. For more on Treaty 7, see Treaty Seven Elders, 1996.

REFERENCES

Adams, C. (2014). Troubling bodies: "The Canadian girl," the ice rink, and the Banff Winter Carnival. *Journal of Canadian Studies, 48(3),* 200-220.

Adams, M. (2006). The game of whose lives? Gender, race, and entitlement in Canada's "national game." In D. Whitson and R. Gruneau (Eds.), *Artificial ice: Hockey, Culture, and commerce.* Peterborough: Broadview Press.

Alfred, T., and Corntassel, J. (2005). Being Indigenous: Resurgences against contemporary colonialism. *Government and Opposition, 40(4),* 596-614.

Anderson, C. & Denis, C. (2004) Urban Natives and the nation: Before and after the Royal Commission on Aboriginal Peoples. *Canadian Review of Sociology and Anthropology, 40(4),* 373-390.

Arellano, A., and Downey, A. (2019). Sport-for-development and the failture of Aboriginal subjecthood: Re-imagining lacrosse as resurgence in Indigenous communities. *Settler Colonial Studies, 9(4),* 457-478. DOI: 10.1080/2201473X.2018.1537078

Belanger, Y., and Laurendeau, J. (2002). Council needs to take a more compassionate approach to homelessness. *Lethbridge Herald,* August 3, 2022. https://www.pressreader.com/canada/lethbridge-herald/20220803/281646783899912

Carlson-Manathara, E. (2021). Settler Colonialism and resistance. In E. Carlson-Manathara & G. Rowe (Eds.), *Living in Indigenous sovereignty* (pp. 28-59). Halifax & Winnipeg: Fernwood Publishing.

Chen, C. (2021a). (Un)making the international student a settler of colour: A decolonising autoethnography. *Qualitative Research in Sport, Exercise and Health, 13(5), 743-762.* DOI: 10.1080/2159676X.2020.1850513.

Chen, C., Mason, D., and Misener, L. (2022). Exploring media coverage of the 2017 World Indigenous Nations Games and North American Indigenous Games: A critical discourse analysis. *Event Management, 22(6),* 1009-1025.

Crosby, A., & Monaghan, J. (2016). Settler colonialism and the policing of Idle No More. *Social Justice, 43(2),* 37-57.

Davies, W. (2020). *Native hoops: The rise of American Indian basketball, 1895-1970.* Lawrence, KS: University Press of Kansas.

Downey, A. (2018). *The Creator's game: Lacrosse, identity, and Indigenous nationhood.* Vancouver, BC: UBC Press.

Dutta, M. (2018). Autoethnography as decolonization, decolonizing autoethnography: Resisting to build our homes. *Cultural Studies ⇔ Critical Methodologies, 18(1),* 94-96. DOI: 10.1177/1532708617735637.

Essa, M., Arellano, A., Stuart, S., and Sheps, S. (2022). Sport for Indigenous resurgence: Toward a critical settler-colonial reflection. *International Review for the Sociology of Sport, 57(2)*, 292-312.

Flowers, R. (2015). Refusal to forgive: Indigenous women's love and rage. *Decolonization: Indigeneity, Education & Society, 4(2),* 32-49.

Forsyth, J. (2013). Bodies of meaning: Sports and games at Canadian residential schools. In J. Forsyth & A. Giles (Eds.), *Aboriginal peoples & sport in Canada* (pp. 15–34). Vancouver, BC: UBC Press.

Forsyth, J. (2020). *Reclaiming Tom Longboat: Indigenous self-determination in Canadian sport.* Regina: University of Regina Press.

Fortier, C., & Wong, E. (2019). The settler colonialism of social work and the social work of settler colonialism. *Settler Colonial Studies, 9(4),* 437-456. DOI: 10.1080/2201473X.2018.1519962.

Giles, A. (2008). Beyond "add women and stir": Politics, feminist development, and dene games. *Leisure, 32(2),* 489-512.

Gilley, B. (2017). The case for colonialism. *Third World Quarterly**

Grande, S. (2018). Refusing the university. In E. Tuck and K. Wayne Yang (Eds.) *Toward what justice? Diverse dreams of justice in education* (pp. 47-65). New York: Routledge.

Grunow, T., Nakamura, F., Hirano, K., Ishihara, M., lewallen, e., Lightfoot, S., Mayunkiki, Medak-Saltzman, D., Williams-Davidson, T., and Yahata, T. (2019). Hokkaidō 150: Settler colonialism and Indigeneity in modern Japan and beyond. *Critical Asian Studies, 51(4),* 597-636.

Hampton, R. (2020). *Black Racialization and Resistance at an Elite University.* Toronto, ON: University of Toronto Press.

Harris, H. (2002). Coyote goes to school: The paradox of Indigenous higher education. *Canadian Journal of Native Education, 26(2),* 187-196.

Heine, M. (2014). No 'museum piece': Aboriginal games and cultural contestation in subarctic Canada. In C. Hullinan & B. Judd (Eds.), *Native games: Indigenous peoples and sports in the post-colonial world* (pp. 1–19). United Kingdom: Emerald.

Hirano, K. (2015). Thanatopolitics in the making of Japan's Hokkaido: Settler colonialism and primitive accumulation. *Critical Historical Studies, 2,* 191-218.

Hunt, D. (2018). "In search of our better selves": Totem transfer narratives and Indigenous futurities. *American Indian Culture and Research Journal, 42(1),* 71-90. DOI: 10.17953/aicrj.42.1.hunt.

Jacobs, M. (2022). "You should be proud!" Native-themed mascots and the cultural reproduction of white settler space. *Sociological Inquiry, 92(2),* 417-441.

Justice, D. (2018). *Why Indigenous literatures matter.* Waterloo: Wilfred Laurier University Press.

Kennedy, L., Silva, D., Coelho, M., & Cipolli, W., III. (2019). "We are all Broncos": Hockey, tragedy, and the formation of Canadian identity. *Sociology of Sport Journal, 36*(3), 189–202. https://doi.org/10.1123/ssj.2019-0006

King, C. R. (2008). Hostile environments: Anti-Indian imagery, racial pedagogies, and youth sport cultures. In M. Giardina & M. Donnelly (Eds.) *Youth culture and sport: Identity, power, and politics* (pp. 147–160). New York: Routledge.

King, C. (2016). Redskins*: Insult and brand.* Lincoln: University of Nebraska Press.

Kulchyski, P. (1992). Primitive subversions: Totalization and resistance in Native Canadian politics. *Cultural Critique, 21,* 171-195.

Kuokkanen, R. (2020). The Deatnu Agreement: A contemporary wall of settler colonialism. *Settler Colonial Studies,10:4,* 508-528, DOI: 10.1080/2201473X.2020.1794211

Ladner, K., & Simpson, L. (2010). Introduction. In L. Simpson & K. Ladner (Eds.) *This is an honour song: Twenty years after the barricades.* Winnipeg, MB: ARP Books.

Laurendeau, J. (2020). "The stories that will make a difference aren't the easy ones": Outdoor recreation, the wilderness ideal, and complicating settler mobility. *Sociology of Sport Journal, 37*(2), 85–95. DOI: 10.1123/ssj.2019-0128.

Laurendeau, J. (2023). *Sport, physical activity, and anti-colonial autoethnography: Stories and ways of being.* London: Routledge.

Leonard, K., Welch, N., and Ali-Joseph, A. (2021). COVID-19 in Indigenous communities: Five protective factors of "exercising" sovereignty. In P. Pedersen, B. Ruihley & B. Li (Eds.), *Sport and the pandemic: Perspectives on COVID-19's impact on the sport industry* (pp. 236-246). London: Routledge.

Lindstrom, G., & Choate, P. (2016). Nistawatsiman: Rethinking assessment of Aboriginal parents for child welfare following the Truth and Reconciliation Commission. *First Peoples Child & Family Review, 11(2),* 45-59.

Liu, L. (2021). Paddling through bluespaces: Understanding waka ama as a post-sport through Indigenous Māori perspectives. *Journal of Sport and Social Issues, 45(2),* 138-160.

MacDonald, D. (2019). *The sleeping giant awakes: Genocide, Indian residential schools, and the challenge of conciliation.* Toronto: University of Toronto Press.

McDonald, M. (2020). Once more, with feeling: Sport, national anthems, and the collective power of affect. *Sociology of Sport Journal, 37(1),* 1-11.

Macoun, A. (2016). Colonising white innocence: Complicity and critical encounters. In S. Maddison, T. Clark, and R. de Costa (Eds.), *The limits of settler colonial reconciliation: Non-Indigenous people and the responsibility to engage* (pp. 85-102). Singapore: Springer.

Mason, C. (2014). *Spirits of the Rockies: Reasserting an Indigenous presence in Banff National Park.* Toronto: University of Toronto Press.

Mason, C., Carr, A., Vandermale, E., Snow, B., & Phillip, L. (2022). Rethinking the role of Indigenous knowledge in sustainable mountain development and protected area management in Canada and Aotearoa/New Zealand. *Mountain Research and Development, 42(4),* A1-A9.

McGuire-Adams, T. (2020). *Indigenous feminist gikendaasowin (knowledge): Decolonization through physical activity.* Palgrave MacMillan.

McGuire-Adams, T. (2021). Settler allies are made, not self-proclaimed: Unsettling conversations for non-Indigenous researchers and educators involved in Indigenous health. *Health Education Journal, 80(7),* 761-772.

McGuire-Adams, T., and Giles, A. (2018). Anishinaabekweg dibaajimowinan (stories) of decolonization through running. *Sociology of Sport Journal, 35,* 207-215.

McKegney, S. (2013). "Pain, pleasure, shame. Shame.": Masculine embodiment, kinship and indigenous reterritorialization. *Canadian Literature, 216,* 12-33.

McKegney, S., Henry, R., Koch, J., & Rathwell, M. (2021). Manufacturing compliance with anti-Indigenous racism in Canadian hockey: The case of Beardy's Blackhawks. *Canadian Ethnic Studies, 53(3),* 29-50. DOI: 10.1353/ces.2021.0017.

Melamed, J. (2015). Racial capitalism. *Critical Ethnic Studies, 1(1),* 76-85.

Norman, M., Hart, M., and Petherick, L. (2019). Indigenous gender reformations: Physical culture, settler colonialism, and the politics of containment. *Sociology of Sport Journal, 36,* 113-123. DOI: https://doi.org/10.1123/ssj.2018-0130.

Norman, M., Petherick, L., and Albert, E. (2022). Unsettling the myth of Canadian nationhood: Hockey and embodied Indigenous sovereignties. *Sociology of Sport Journal, 39(4),* 323-332. DOI: https://doi.org/10.1123/ssj.2021-0115

O'Bonsawin, C. (2010). "No Olympics on stolen native land": contesting Olympic narratives and asserting indigenous rights within the discourse of the 2010 Vancouver Games. *Sport in Society, 13(1),* 143-156. DOI: 10.1080/17430430903377987.

O'Bonsawin, C. (2017). "Ready to step up and hold the front line": Transitioning from Sport History to Indigenous Studies, and back again. *The International Journal of the History of Sport, 34,(5-6),* 420-426. DOI: 10.1080/09523367.2017.1378184.

O'Bonsawin, C. (2021). The assertion of Canada's colonial self in national and international sport. In C. Adams (Ed.), *Sport and recreation in Canadian history* (pp. 275-302).

Olive, R., & Wheaton, B. (2021). Understanding blue spaces: Sport, bodies, wellbeing, and the sea. *Journal of Sport and Social Issues, 45(1),* 3-19.

Paraschak, V., and Heine, M. (2020). Co-transforming through shared understandings of land-based practices in sport for development and peace. In: R. Millington and S. Darnell (Eds.) *Sport, development and environmental sustainability* (pp. 178–194). London: Routledge.

Puwar, N. (2004). *Space invaders: Race, gender, and bodies out of place.* Oxford: Berg.

Pyne, S. (2014). Sound of the drum, energy of the dance – making the Lake Huron Treaty Atlas the Anishinaabe way. Unpublished Ph.D. Dissertation. Carleton University.

Robinson, D. (2016). International sense, intergenerational responsibility. In D. Robinson & K. Martin (Eds.), *Arts of engagement: Taking aesthetic action in and beyond the truth and reconciliation commission of Canada* (pp. 43–65). Waterloo: Wilfred Laurier University Press.

Rodriguez, A. (2018). A case against colonialism. *Postcolonial Studies, 21(2),* 254-259.

Scherer, J., Davidson, J., Kafara, R., & Koch, J. (2021). Negotiating the new urban sporting territory: Policing, settler colonialism, and Edmonton's ice district. *Sociology of Sport Journal, 38(2),* 111-119.

Sharrow, E., Tarsi, M., and Nteta, T. (2021). What's in a name? Symbolic racism, public opinion, and the controversy over the NFL's Washington football team name. *Race and Social Problems, 13*, 110-121.

Shihade, M. (2017). Sports and politics in Israel: Settler colonialism and the native Palestinians. In N. Koch (Ed.), *Critical geographies of sport: Space, power, and sport in global perspective* (pp. 64-74). London: Routledge.

Skogvang, B. (2021). Sámi sports and life at the indigenous Riddu Riđđu festival. *Journal of Adventure Education and Outdoor Learning, 21(4),* 357-370.

Simpson, A. (2017). The ruse of consent and the anatomy of 'refusal': cases from indigenous North America and Australia. *Postcolonial Studies, 20(1),* 18-33. DOI: 10.1080/13688790.2017.1334283.

Simpson, L. (2011). *Dancing on our turtle's back: Stories of Nishnaabeg re-creation, resurgence, and a new emergence.* Winnipeg: Arbeiter Ring Publishing.

Simpson, L. (2014). Land as pedagogy: Nishnaabeg intelligence and rebellious transformation. *Decolonization: Indigeneity, Education & Society, 3(3),* 1-25.

Simpson, L. (2017). *As we have always done: Indigenous freedom through radical resistance.* Minneapolis: University of Minnesota Press.

Slater, L. (2019). *Anxieties of belonging in settler colonialism: Australia, race and place.* New York: Routledge.

Slater, L. (2020). A politics of uncertainty: Good white people, emotions, and political responsibility. *Continuum, 34(6),* 816-827. DOI: 10.1080/10304312.2020.1842122.

Spence, M. (1999). *Dispossessing the wilderness: Indian removal and the making of the national parks.* New York: Oxford University Press.

Stewart, T. (2021). What does it mean to "stand on guard for thee"? Detuning the Canadian national anthem. Unpublished M.A. Thesis. University of Lethbridge.

Stonechild, B. (2006). *The new buffalo: The struggle for Aboriginal post-secondary education in Canada.* Winnipeg: University of Manitoba Press.

Strakosch, E. (2015). *Neoliberal Indigenous policy: Settler colonialism and the "post-welfare" state.* New York: Palgrave Macmillan.

Tuck, E. (2009). Suspending damage: A letter to communities. *Harvard Educational Review, 79(3),* 409-427.

Tuck, E., & Yang, K. (2012). Decolonization is not a metaphor. *Decolonization: Indigeneity, Education & Society, 1(1),* 1-40.

Vander Kloet (2009). A trip to the co-op: The production, consumption, and salvation of Canadian wilderness. *International Journal of Canadian Studies, 39/40,* 231–251. DOI: 10.7202/040831ar.

Veracini, L. (2011). Introducing settler colonial studies. *Settler Colonial Studies, 1(1),* 1-12.

Waiti, J., & Awatere, S. (2019). Kaihekengaru: Māori surfers and a sense of place. *Journal of Coastal Research, SI 87,* 35-43.

Waiti, J., & Wheaton, B. (2022). Culture: Indigenous Māori knowledges of the ocean and leisure practices. In K. Peters, J. Anderson, A. Davies, & P. Steinberg (Eds.), *The Routledge Handbook of Ocean Space* (pp. 85-100). London: Routledge.

Whitinui, P. (2014). Indigenous autoethnography: Exploring, engaging, and experiencing "self" as a narrative method of inquiry. *Journal of Contemporary Ethnography, 43(4)*, 456-487. DOI: 10.1177/0891241613508148.

Wigglesworth, J. (2021). The cultural politics of naming outdoor climbing routes. *Annals of Leisure Research, 22(5),* 597-620.

Wikaire, R., and Newman, J. (2013). Neoliberalism as neocolonialism? Considerations on the marketization of waka ama in Aotearoa/New Zealand. In C. Hallihan and B. Judd (Eds.), *Native games: Indigenous peoples and sports in the post-colonial world* (pp. 59-83). Bingley: Emerald.

Wolfe, P. (2006). Settler colonialism and the elimination of the native. *Journal of Genocide Research, 8(4),* 387-409. DOI: 10.1080/14623520601056240.

Woolford, A. (2014). Discipline, territory, and the colonial mesh: Indigenous boarding schools in the United States and Canada. In A. Woolford, J. Benvenuto, and A. Hinton (Eds.), *Colonial genocide in Indigenous North America* (pp. 29-47). Durham: Duke University Press.

Woolford, A. (2015). *This benevolent experiment: Indigenous boarding schools, genocide, and redress in Canada and the United States.* Lincoln: University of Nebraska Press.

LINKS FOR REPOSITORY

Hurley, L. (2022). "Conservative Supreme Court Justices question Native American adoption law." *NBC News*, https://www.nbcnews.com/politics/supreme-court/supreme-court-weighs-challenge-native-american-adoption-law-rcna55574

Reconciliation Australia (n.d.). "Truth-telling." https://www.reconciliation.org.au/our-work/truth-telling/

Royal Commission on Aboriginal Peoples (1996). "Report of the Royal Commission on Aboriginal Peoples." https://www.bac-lac.gc.ca/eng/discover/aboriginal-heritage/royal-commission-aboriginal-peoples/Pages/introduction.aspx

Statistics Canada, "Indigenous Population Continues to Grow and is Much Younger than the Non-Indigenous Population, Although the Pact of Growth has Slowed," September 9, 2022, https://www150.statcan.gc.ca/n1/daily-quotidien/220921/dq220921a-eng.htm.

Truth and Reconciliation Commission of Canada. (2015). "Honouring the truth, reconciling for the future." https://ehprnh2mwo3.exactdn.com/wp-content/uploads/2021/01/Executive_Summary_English_Web.pdf

Truth and Reconciliation Commission of Canada. (n.d.). "Sports and reconciliation." https://www.rcaanc-cirnac.gc.ca/eng/1524505883755/1557512006268

Waterton Lakes National Park. (n.d.). "Waterton Lakes visitor centre." https://parks.canada.ca/pn-np/ab/waterton/activ/accueil-visitor

www.ingramcontent.com/pod-product-compliance
Lightning Source LLC
Chambersburg PA
CBHW022132160426
43197CB00009B/1253